SCALE SYSTEM FOR RELUCTANT SCALE ENTHUSIASTS

FOR VIOLIN

OLGA DUBOSSARSKAYA KALER

SCALE SYSTEM FOR RELUCTANT SCALE ENTHUSIASTS

FOR VIOLIN

OLGA DUBOSSARSKAYA KALER

Scale System for Reluctant Scale Enthusiasts
For Violin
by Olga Dubossarskaya Kaler

Cover Design: Maria Camoletto
Text Edit: Meghan Henson
Music Edit and Layout: Rasa Mahmoudian

2nd Edition 2019
Digital Edition 2019: Ovation Press, Ltd.
1st Edition 2015

Copyright © 2019 Olga Dubossarskaya Kaler
All rights reserved.
ISBN 978-1-695-14246-6

Dedicated to Vadim Gluzman:

great violinist, admired colleague, and dear friend.

Praised by critics for her "deep, soulful sound" and "powerful, enchanting renditions," Olga Dubossarskaya Kaler has toured three continents as a soloist, chamber musician, and artist-teacher, having combined performing and teaching careers with equal success. She is a member of the violin faculty at the Cleveland Institute of Music, following a 15-year tenure as a violin professor at the DePaul University School of Music in Chicago.

As a member of the World Orchestra for Peace under the direction of Valery Gergiev, Kaler has appeared on some of the world's most legendary concert stages, including the Carnegie Hall of New York, the Moscow Conservatory Great Hall, the Albert Hall of London, and the Berlin Philharmonie Hall, to name a few. In addition, Kaler performs regularly with the Chautauqua Symphony Orchestra of New York and The Chicago Ensemble.

Kaler has received numerous awards as a performer, including the Special Prize at the Rodolfo Lipizer International Competition, and first prizes at the Northwestern and Thaviu-Isaak Competitions. Her previous orchestral engagements include the Chicago Symphony, the Boston Symphony, and the Indianapolis Symphony Orchestra. She has held leadership positions with the Rochester Philharmonic Orchestra, the Ars Viva Orchestra of Chicago, and the Syracuse Symphony Orchestra.

Highly sought-after as an artist-teacher and guest clinician, she has presented masterclasses at the Eastman School of Music, Northwestern University, Michigan State University, and Andrews University, among others. Her summer festival teaching and performance engagements have included the International Heifetz Institute, the Keshet Eilon International String Mastercourse, the Bowdoin International Music Festival in Maine, the Skaneateles Music Festival in New York, the North Shore Chamber Music Festival in Chicago, and the Montreal Festival in Canada, to name a few.

Kaler's students regularly place in competitions throughout the United States and abroad. The Gold Medal at the Rotary Club of Europe competition is among their recent achievements, as well as awards at the Sony Young Artist International Competition, the National Opera Society Competition, the Fischoff National Chamber Music Competition, the Saint Paul String Quartet Competition, the Discover Chamber Music Competition, the Rembrandt Competition, and the Stradivari Competition of Italy.

Her recent works of scholarship, *Scale System for Reluctant Scale Enthusiasts* and *An Effective Method for Teaching and Studying Violin Technique*, have been met with enthusiastic reception from string players and pedagogues worldwide. Both textbooks have been adopted into pedagogy curriculums and added to library materials at major conservatories in the United States and abroad.

Kaler holds a Doctor of Musical Arts from the Northwestern University Bienen School of Music, as well as previous degrees from the New England Conservatory of Boston, the Moscow State Conservatory in Russia, and the Stolyarsky Special Music School for Gifted Children in Odessa, Ukraine. Her most influential teachers include Almita Vamos, Nelli Shkolnikova, Benjamin Mordkovich, Naoum Latinsky, Inna Gaukhman, and James Buswell.

For more information visit: http://www.olgadkaler.com.

Acknowledgements

I would like to express my infinite gratitude to two people without whom this project would not have been possible: Meghan Henson, for her help in editing the text, and Rasa Mahmoudian, for helping to edit and prepare the Finale files for this work.

My thanks continue to those who contributed to the first edition of this work: Andrew Miller, for his help with Finale and logistical support, and Alyssa Mathias and Dara Miller for their help with editing the text.

I also extend my deepest gratitude to my greatest source of inspiration: my husband, Ilya Kaler, for his unfailing support and shared belief in the profound importance of this work.

TABLE OF CONTENTS

Preface x

How to Use This Book xi

Learning and Maintaining Proper Technique xii

A Note on Scale Fingerings xiv

A Guide to Bow Strokes xv

Pizzicato Scale xxvi

From Slow to Fast: The Use of Vibrato in Scales and Rhythmic Accelerations xxviii

3 Octave Scales and Arpeggios

G Major/G Minor 3

Ab Major/Ab Minor 8

A Major/A Minor 13

Bb Major/Bb Minor 18

B Major/B Minor 23

C Major/C Minor 28

Db Major/C# Minor 33

D Major/D Minor 38

Eb Major/Eb Minor 43

E Major/E Minor 48

F Major/F Minor 53

F# Major/F# Minor 58

4 Octave Scales and Arpeggios

G Major/G Minor 65

Ab Major/Ab Minor 68

A Major/A Minor.. 71

Bb Major/Bb Minor 74

B major/B Minor 77

PREFACE

This scale system is intended for use by advanced violin students, professional violinists, and teachers alike. It addresses the same needs as the methods of Galamian and Flesch but differs in the way that the scales are organized, including suggestions for bow technique and vibrato maintenance, as well as new techniques not found in other systems. Also included is an ornamented scale that incorporates the trill element into scale work; not only does it improve finger dexterity but helps to develop coordination for passagework in repertoire. The ornamented scale in thirds presents significant challenges to the performer and helps to develop awareness of slurred string crossings while also executing consecutive shifts. It is particularly challenging in the keys where the use of open strings is not possible, but the benefit of incorporating these scales into one's practice routine is indisputable. This is clearly demonstrated by Mr. Heifetz, who used ornamented scales in thirds in his own daily practice. These scales help to further one's knowledge of the fingerboard and to improve the overall sense of intonation.

Time constraints often prevent many musicians of our generation from focusing on developing and maintaining their technique through the careful practice of scales. With this in mind, I have created this scale system based on over twenty years of my own teaching and performing. This system allows a violinist to go through all major and minor scales within a period of twelve days. Using this system, a violinist who has reached a complete level of comfort with the scales at the suggested speeds will require no more than half an hour per day to go through all of the techniques suggested here twice, including bow strokes, double-stops, and harmonics.

In my recently published work, *An Effective Method For Teaching And Studying Violin Technique*, I focused on dissecting and analyzing each individual violin technique and created a system of developmental exercises leading up to a level to which this scale system is the next logical step.

How to Use This Book

To ensure proper technique, scales should be introduced as soon as the student is ready to combine the left hand with the bow. Most young students will resent playing scales and will be bored unless the teacher is able to constantly reference the repertoire that the scales are intended to support. If technical studies are disconnected from their true purpose — providing the necessary tools for music-making — they become meaningless sources of suffering for students, parents, and teachers alike. This scale system will deepen the connection between technical exercises and repertoire, sparing teachers from attempts to preach the virtue of daily routines which may otherwise seem insufferable.

Before assigning any scale, etude, or exercise, the teacher should explain its purpose and the set of skills that it intends to teach. It is helpful to give an example of a specific piece of music that each particular set of exercises will make possible to perform. More importantly, the teacher should make the concept of constant maintenance clear; just as a great athlete that won the Olympic Gold medal would not be able to repeat this achievement without maintaining and improving upon his or her skills, so is a performing artist only as good as he or she is today. Training our muscles to perform certain tasks is necessary in order to develop the tools for music-making and requires the same discipline as that of an athlete. All performing musicians must acquire an incredible amount of knowledge about the way their bodies work. However, our profession is not strictly knowledge-based but rather depends on our ability to apply that knowledge toward acquiring new skills. It is an exciting but endless process, combining physical, intellectual, and emotional abilities. This remains a universal truth not only for beginners but for artists of the highest caliber.

Learning and Maintaining Proper Technique

Playing in an orchestra, chamber group, or even as a soloist is not sufficient to remain in perfect instrumental form. Many great violinists of the past took time off from their busy performance schedules every summer to go over each aspect of their technique. This regular maintenance gave them the discipline to survive the demands of their careers for decades. Unfortunately, many violinists today do not know where to begin this important work. The technical reserves one builds and maintains over the course of one's career are easily depleted without proper discipline and maintenance. The list below should help any violinist or teacher to monitor some of the vital aspects of violin technique that can be practiced using this scale system:

I. **Sound production** should always be practiced with a specific goal in mind. For example, one may work toward building bow control by holding notes for durations of up to twenty beats. Alternatively, one may work on dynamics by using specific bow speeds in each part of the bow. To help with the concept of bow distribution, one may use the metronome to fit a predetermined number of beats within each section of the bow. No matter the goal, the sound should always be even and clear.

II. **Finger dexterity** should be adjusted to tempo: the slower the tempo, the more distance there should be between the finger and the fingerboard. However slowly one plays, the finger should be lifted and lowered quickly at a uniform angle, with the pad of the fingertip in front of the nail. As the tempo increases, the distance will decrease, but the speed of the falling finger should not change. Take care to keep all of the fingers over the fingerboard so that no additional adjustment is needed to bring the 3rd and 4th fingers down. Training the hand correctly at a slow tempo will prepare it for an immediate and effortless tempo increase.

III. **String crossings** should be done with both hands and require constant monitoring. In ascending motion, the last finger used on the previous string should remain down until the next finger is securely placed on the higher string. In descending motion, the 4th finger should be placed on the lower string while the 1st finger is being played on the upper string. These preparations not only help to conceal the string crossings but ensure precise intonation, as well. Additionally, the bow arm should stay slightly ahead of each string crossing. This facilitates a single motion across all four strings rather than a series of jerky movements from string to string. Crossing down to the higher strings should be led by the upper arm, while the motion up toward the lower strings should be led by the right wrist, followed by the rest of the arm.

IV. **Bow arm level** should be adjusted in advance toward the level of the new string. The bow should gradually approach each new string level, creating the illusion of playing on a single string and masking all string crossings.

V. **Vibrato** should be developed and maintained with scales. When working on dynamics, it is beneficial to add vibrato to long notes with changing bow speeds, coordinating the vibrato speed and width to the speed of the bow. Similarly, playing a slow, slurred scale will help to reinforce constant and even vibrato, passing it from finger to finger and keeping the motion consistent during shifts.

VI. **Bow strokes** should constitute the technical arsenal of every violinist and should be maintained on scales.

VII. **Double-stops** should always be included in scale work. In this scale system, major/minor thirds, sixths, octaves, and fingered octaves are presented, as well a valuable ornamented thirds exercise inspired by Jascha Heifetz. A scale in **harmonics** completes the daily routine.

A Note on Scale Fingerings

The choice of fingerings stems from my own performance experience and learning through trial and error what is most reliable under pressure. I strove to offer consistent fingerings, making it relatively easy to apply these patterns to any group of scales. I also aimed to provide the best possible fingering option for passages that may appear in repertoire.

The three-octave scales have different sets of fingerings for the lower (Ab-B) and upper (C-F#) Major and Minor scales. With the exception of the G scales, the lower three-octave scales share the same fingering principle: all begin on the 1st finger and employ one ascending shift on the A string with the remaining shifts performed on the E string. When later studied as four-octave scales, this fingering will help to divide up a long series of shifts that one would otherwise need if waiting to start shifting until the E string. The remaining upper scales start on the 2nd finger and have their first ascending shift on the E string. This achieves two objectives: first, to teach the skill of gradually moving into higher positions with each subsequent scale, and second, to demonstrate the left hand's role in string crossings in areas of the instrument where the strings become increasingly higher. My choice of fingerings in arpeggios is based on consistency and comfort, which are most likely to produce the best results in terms of technical stability and sound quality. Another objective in having two fingering concepts is to prepare the hand for any fingering requirement in both triplet and quadruplet patterns.

Should any additional details be desired to aid in the complete understanding of the various technical challenges of violin playing, my earlier work *An Effective Method For Teaching And Studying Violin Technique* will resolve many questions.

A Guide to Bow Strokes

Martelé

This stroke is executed in the upper half and uses a fast bow speed. When practicing *martelé*, the breaks between notes should equal the value of the note itself. As with any other stroke that employs a fast bow speed, *martelé* should not be played near the bridge, and the position of the left hand should be used to determine the amount of bow to be used. The shorter the string, the slower the bow speed will be needed, thus a higher register on each string will require less bow.

1. Set the bow in the middle. Keep the upper left arm motionless.
2. Pronate the forearm to apply its weight onto the bow through the index finger.
3. Once the string is well engaged, pull the bow using a very fast speed, feeling a horizontal pull sensation. Be sure not to release until after the bow is in motion.
4. Allow the bow to come to a complete stop. There is no separate motion to stop the bow; the only effort exerted should go toward beginning the next stroke in the new direction.
5. The amount of the bow to be used depends on the hight of ones forearm, which must open, the bow placement, and the tilt of the stick.

— listen to some Viotti

Viotti Stroke

This stroke consists of two hooked *martelé* notes, with the second note accented. When practicing this stroke on scales, the first note of the scale should be played as a single note, with all subsequent notes hooked. The first hooked note is played *martelé* in the upper half, using only one to two inches of bow. The second hooked note should take almost the entire length of the upper half. Each note should be attacked with equal energy, allowing the fast bow speed (and subsequently, greater length) of the second note to produce the accent.

XV

Dotted ("Shoe Shine") Stroke

The dotted stroke is performed in the upper half using no more than one-eighth of the bow. Most of the energy in executing this stroke goes into the down-bow note. Similar to the *martelé* stroke, the index finger suppresses the bow, followed by a quick counter-clockwise, rotational motion in the right hand initiated by the right thumb. The role of the forearm here is very minimal, as it mainly follows the wrist. The up-bow note is performed primarily on the release of the bow without any further involvement from the hand. The amount of bow used will depend on the tempo.

1. Place the bow at the tip or in the middle of the upper half.
2. Play a short up-bow eighth note.
3. Pronate the forearm to apply its weight through the index finger onto the bow.
4. Similarly, feel the counterpressure of the thumb against the frog.
5. Play a quick down-bow sixteenth note, pulling with the thumb. Keep the index finger engaged. The hand will move in an active counter-counterclockwise motion.
6. Allow the hand to bounce back on its own on the up-bow, simply by relaxing it.
7. Prepare the new finger as quickly as possible during the rest.
8. Repeat the scale starting the first note on a down-bow (begin with step three).

Collé

Start this exercise by playing only on the string. Once satisfied with the sound quality and ease of execution, this stroke can be performed off-the-string, as well. Each stroke should last as long as the length of the fingers will allow, even in the off-the-string version. Avoid applying excessive pressure, which can create a rough and choked sound. Once in motion, the bow should move lightly at a high speed.

1. Set the bow directly above the winding in the middle of the lower half.
2. Keep the hand flattened and the fingers flexed, especially the pinky.
3. Employing finger motion only, move down-bow. To ensure the movement is being performed correctly, practice holding the bow vertically, using the fingers to move it up and down. The bow should be propelled primarily by the up and down motion of the thumb. Watching the tip is helpful in order to determine if the finger movement is moving the bow in a strictly vertical fashion (as it should be), or simply swaying it side to side.
4. Stop the bow and rest for a duration equal to the note played.
5. Reset the bow into the string and flex the fingers in order to travel up-bow.

Frog-Tip

This exercise can be thought of as a series of whole bow *martelé* notes, with part of the note played above the string. Maintain an even bow speed and stay as close to the string as possible when changing bow placement.

1. Set the bow at the frog.
2. Play a short note on a down-bow using about one-eighth of the bow.
3. Lift the bow without stopping, moving above the string toward the tip.
4. Reset the bow at the tip.
5. Play a short note on an up-bow using about one-eighth of the bow.
6. Lift the bow without stopping, moving above the string toward the frog.

Reverse Frog-Tip

This stroke is similar to Frog-Tip, but with reversed bow directions. The first stroke is performed in the lower half as an up-bow *collé* and the second note *martelé* in the upper half. As in Frog-Tip, the bow moves above the string during the rest to a different part of the bow. This exercise is an excellent tool for learning bow control when a quick change in bow placement is required.

1. Set the bow in the lower quarter of the bow, with the fingers extended.
2. Perform an up-bow *collé* stroke, lifting off of the string after the fingers are fully flexed.
3. Balancing the bow between the thumb, index finger, and pinky, move the bow above the string toward the tip, resetting in the middle of the upper half.
4. Engage the string and perform a down-bow *martelé* stroke.
5. After playing the *martelé* stroke, lift off of the string and move toward the lower half.
6. Reset in the lower quarter of the bow to perform the next up-bow *collé*.

Staccato

For both down-bow and up-bow *staccato*, it is important to keep the right arm passive so that the pressure/release of the index finger can move the bow. The right index finger provides the pressure, while the right thumb provides the counter pressure.

In general, this stroke should not be played near the bridge. However, when used in repertoire, the *staccato* may need to move closer to the bridge in higher position passages. As the bow travels into the upper half, the tilt and angle should change to more of a right angle in relation to the string, and the bow hair should flatten.

For down-bow staccato:
1. Place the bow in the lower half and tilt the stick toward the bridge, pushing the frog away from the body toward the fingerboard. The tip of the bow should be slightly angled toward the bridge, without being exaggerated.

2. Lean into the string with the index finger, and then release, allowing the bow to move slightly. Avoid actively moving the right arm.
3. As you move into the upper half, gradually straighten the bow to become perpendicular with the bridge.

For up-bow staccato:
1. Set the bow in the upper half and tilt the stick away from the bridge, using the outer side of the hair. Pull the frog in slightly toward the body to angle the tip toward the fingerboard, but without exaggeration. The height of the right arm should be above the bow.
2. Lean into the string with the index finger and then release, allowing the bow to move slightly. Avoid actively moving the right arm.
3. Once the above skills have been mastered, the following steps are recommended to increase the tempo:
    a) Practice grouping the notes into sets of two by releasing the index finger only partially after the first *staccato* note, and fully releasing after the second note. It is helpful to pause between units in order to regroup and re-engage the bow for the next pair of *staccato* notes.
    b) Once this concept is fully absorbed, units of three and four *staccato* notes may be introduced.

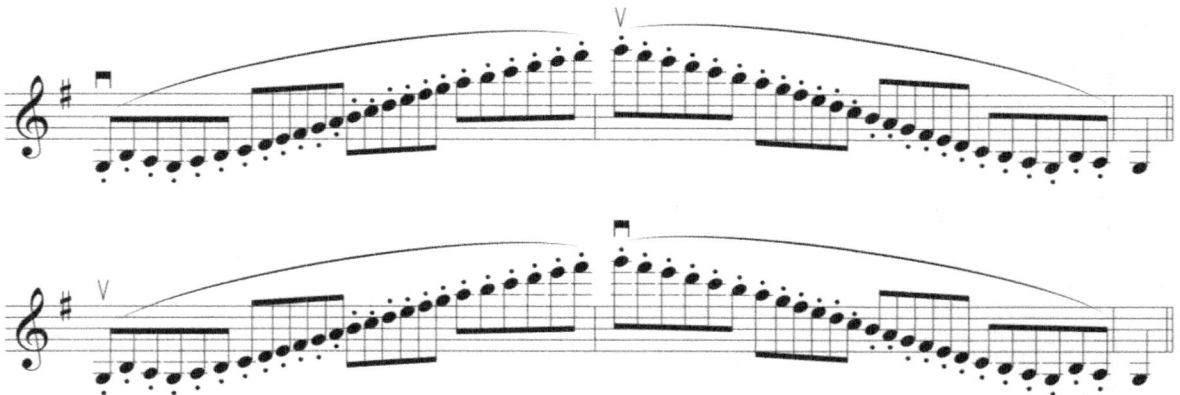

Sautillé

Sautillé is a fast version of the *detaché* stroke, with the bow hair never leaving the string. The stick will begin to bounce at a fast tempo, creating the illusion of an off-the-string stroke. The success of this exercise depends on the careful assessment of each step and the quality of the *detaché*. One should listen for a perfectly even sound and inaudible bow changes. It is imperative that the right-hand fingers and wrist remain relatively uninvolved save for the index finger, which helps keep the bow hair glued to the string at all times. For further instructions regarding the *detaché* stroke, refer to *An Effective Method For Teaching And Studying Violin Technique.*

Every bow is different, so the optimal bow placement for *sautillé* will depend on the individual bow's balance point. It is, however, safe to state that the range for the *sautillé* could be anywhere from the middle of the lower half to the middle of the bow. The faster the tempo, the higher the bow placement for this stroke. If the bow begins to jump excessively, tilt the stick away from the bridge so that it acquires the flexibility to act as a "shock absorber." Similarly, if the stroke is lacking in clarity, flatten the bow hair by tilting the stick slightly toward the bridge to allow it to bounce.

If the sound quality is unsatisfactory at any point during the course of this exercise, return to the previous figure and recover the sound before proceeding to the next subdivision.

1. Using the upper arm, play *detaché* notes in the quarter of the bow directly below the middle. Set the metronome to approximately 100-120 BPM per quarter note. (Fig. A)
2. Switch to quarter note triplets. Reduce the amount of bow to match the sound quality of the previous figure. Continue using the upper arm. (Fig. B)
3. Switch to eighth notes and further reduce the amount of bow. If the tempo is fast enough, the minimal forearm motion will be all that is necessary. (Fig. C)
4. Switch from eighth notes to eighth-note triplets. Further reduce the amount of bow toward the middle and use primarily the forearm and a slight motion of the wrist. Continue playing *detaché*; do not attempt to come off of the string. (Fig. D)
5. Switch to sixteenth notes. Further reduce the amount of bow and keep the stick firmly suppressed with the index finger. Do not allow the bow hair to come off of the string. At this point the stroke should become *sautillé*. (Fig. E)

Once a satisfactory *sautillé* has been obtained, apply this stroke to any given scale by playing each note as a sixteenth-note triplet.

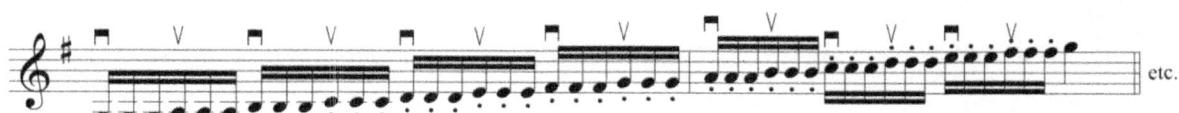

Spiccato

It is important to think of the *spiccato* stroke as an off-the-string *detaché*. This will help to avoid a crunchy beginning to every note. There is no metronome marking assigned to this exercise; rather, one may add more subdivisions to arrive at the desired stroke.

1. Begin *spiccato* work with its parent stroke - *detaché*. Using the upper arm, play *detaché* quarter notes using the quarter of the bow directly below the middle. Aim for pure and even sound quality with inaudible bow changes. (Fig. A)
2. Using a *detaché* motion, play four notes in each direction with a stroke similar to *saltando*, but starting from the string and slightly lifting the bow in between. All notes should be relatively long and uniform and should not sound percussive. Avoid dipping the wrist and do not drop the bow onto the string; anticipate the new direction with the right arm by slightly lifting it just prior to each up-bow change. (Fig. B)
3. Switch to triplets, maintaining the ratio to the original quarter note. Reduce the amount of bow and return to the same part of the bow for each new down-bow group. The vertical arm motion should become more pronounced with each new subdivision (Fig. C)
4. Switch to sixteenths, with two notes in each direction. Further reduce the amount of bow. (Fig. D)
5. Play separate notes, dipping the bow in and out of string. It helps to think of *spiccato* as off-the-string *detaché*. Make the *spiccato* long and aim for a clear, mild sound. Be sure to maintain core to the sound as the tempo increases.

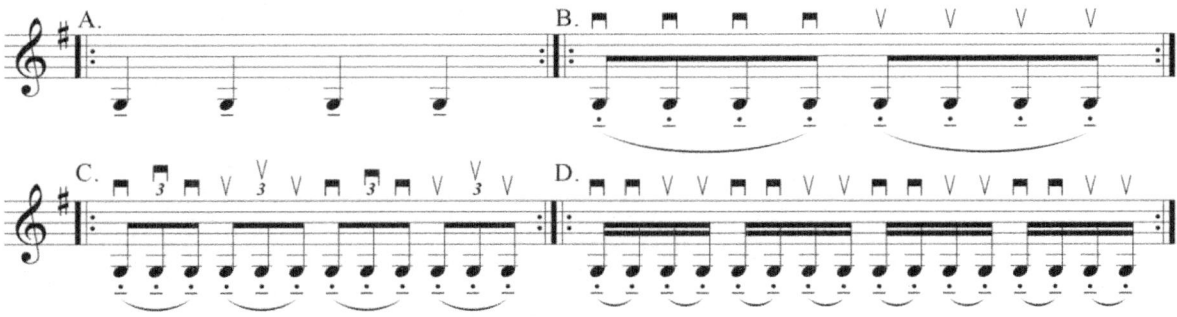

When applying *spiccato* to scales and repertoire, keep in mind that string changes should be done by changing the upper arm level. The bow should be kept close to the string during the string changes and in higher positions, as well, where one must also reduce the amount of bow to accommodate for the increased string tension. Once a satisfactory *spiccato* has been obtained, it may be applied to any scale:

Flying Staccato

To perform this stroke, the right hand should start in a more pronated position (such as when playing in the upper half) with a higher upper arm. Tilt the bow toward the fingerboard to allow it to act as a "shock absorber" and to cushion the landings. Bring the frog slightly in toward the body; this will angle the bow in a way that allows each string to respond equally.

1. Set the bow at the frog, directly above the winding.
2. Play a down-bow *detaché* quarter note, connecting to an up-bow *detaché* eighth note. Stay on the string. (Fig. A)
3. Play a *detaché* quarter note followed by two up-bow eighth notes. Lift the bow off of the string after the second eighth note. Use a smooth up-bow motion preceded by a slight lift in the right elbow. (Fig. B)
4. Hold the bow in a pronated hand position with the fingers dropped down and relaxed.
5. From this position, play a series of up-bow *spiccato* notes, aiming for a uniform and smooth sound. Return to the same part of the bow for each new note. (Fig. C)
6. Move to the triplet pattern. Play a dotted quarter note down-bow followed by three triplet up-bow eighth notes. (Fig. D)
    a. The first of the three eighth notes should be played *detaché* and kept strictly on the string.
    b. The second eighth note should start on the string but lift off.
    c. The third note should be played as an up-bow *spiccato*.
7. Figures E-G may be used to build up the tempo and number of successive flying *staccato* notes. After the third note, each note should be performed as continuous up-bow *spiccato*, returning to the same part of the bow for each stroke (as in Fig. C).

Once a satisfactory flying staccato has been achieved, the following combinations may be used to maintain the stroke on any scale.

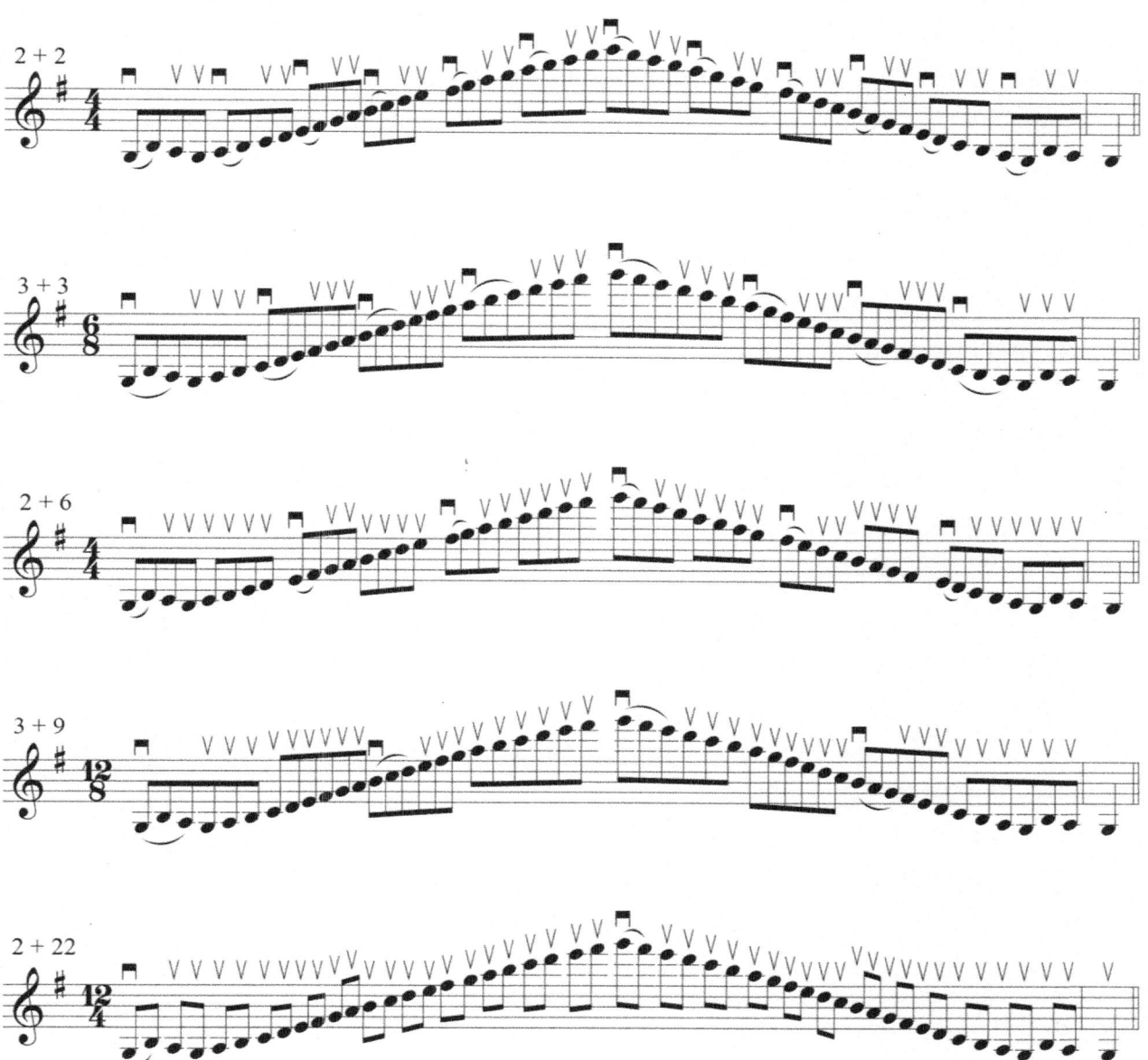

Pizzicato Scales

Of all the techniques necessary to be considered an accomplished instrumentalist, *pizzicato* appears to be one of the most neglected. It is generally assumed that one simply plucks the string and that there is little more to know, though this is far from being the case. Considering how often this technical device is employed in both solo and ensemble repertoire, it is certainly worth including *pizzicato* practice in this scale system alongside other cornerstone string techniques.

Right Hand Pizzicato
Similar to playing *arco*, in which one places the bow on the string and pulls slightly until the string catches, producing the best *pizzicato* sound requires suppressing the string with the pad of the finger until it is brought down to the fingerboard. The string is released as the finger moves at a slightly diagonal angle in the direction of the upper strings. Upward arm gestures in *pizzicato* chords are actually counterproductive; the motion that contributes to the best *pizzicato* sound is one that employs the arm to pull the finger and hand toward the upper strings in a motion that replicates the curve of the bridge.

It is worth noting that some string players prefer to use their right second finger or right thumb instead of the index to perform right-hand *pizzicato*. Two fingers are sometimes employed to perform double-stops or chords. The *pizzicato* sequence in the Fugue from Bartók's Sonata for Solo Violin is one such example. This passage is often performed with a combination of the thumb and second finger, as one must simultaneously pluck notes separated by two octaves on the G and E strings.

Left Hand Pizzicato
This technique should be introduced separately before using it extensively in repertoire. It requires considerable finger strength and some fingertip calluses, which take time to develop. To perform left-hand *pizzicato*, the left arm should be positioned closer to the body, balancing the left hand toward the higher positions. The fingers should be placed relatively flat on the side of the lower string and angled back toward the scroll.

Begin by completely suppressing the string with the finger and pulling it along the fingerboard toward the higher string. The finger should never be brought underneath the string and should not be pulled upward - only sideways. The volume of the *pizz* will increase over time as the strength of the fingers permits. To avoid fingertip blisters, limit practice time for this technique to no more than five minutes per practice session.

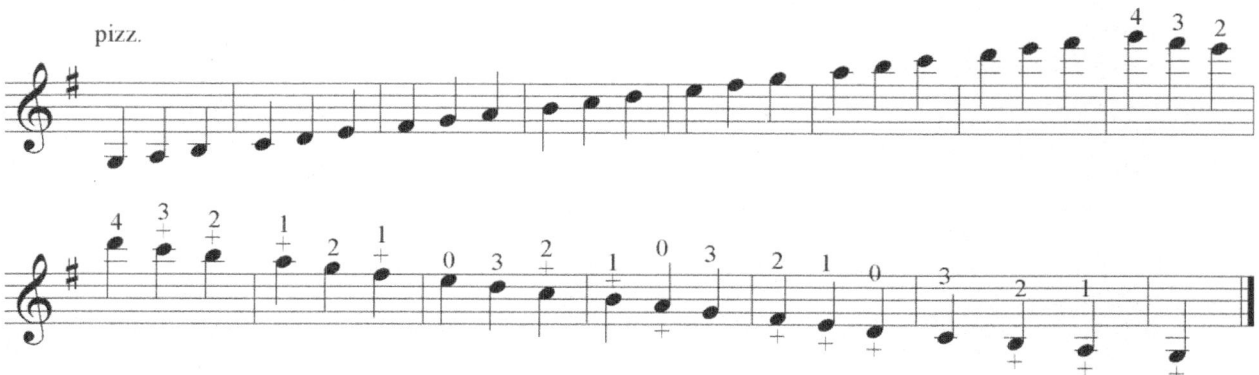

xxvii

From Slow to Fast:
Using Vibrato in Scales and Rhythmic Accelerations

The most efficient way to maintain vibrato technique is to incorporate it into scale practice. This is also a very effective way to warm up the muscles of the left hand.

1. Play a scale at approximately 54 BPM or slower, with one note per bow for four beats each.
2. Start with a very slow bow speed and barely perceptible vibrato (slow and narrow).
3. Fit the first three beats within the lower half of the bow, saving the upper half for the fourth beat.
4. Compensate for the lighter weight at the tip by increasing bow speed. Similarly, increase the width and intensity of the vibrato as the bow speed increases.

The next stage of the scale study process is to play three slurred notes per bow at 35 BPM. This first slurred pattern may be used to maintain vibrato skills. While the previous exercise is excellent for exploring vibrato range, this one is best employed for practicing continuous vibrato. One may monitor the consistency of the vibrato while transitioning to new notes, strings, and positions. To pass vibrato from one finger to another, the previous finger should remain on the string until the next one is placed and vibrating, as well. In descending motion, the new finger should be placed on the string in advance and vibrated with the sounding note.

All subsequent rhythmic accelerations should be performed at 35 BPM per quarter note, altering the number of notes per bow and per beat. It is important to use a slower bow speed in the lower half throughout all scales and for all rhythmic subdivisions, employing the upper half of the bow for fewer notes, which will allow for a slight crescendo toward the tip - a crucial skill that must be developed by all successful performers.

Rhythmic Accelerations
3 Octave Scales

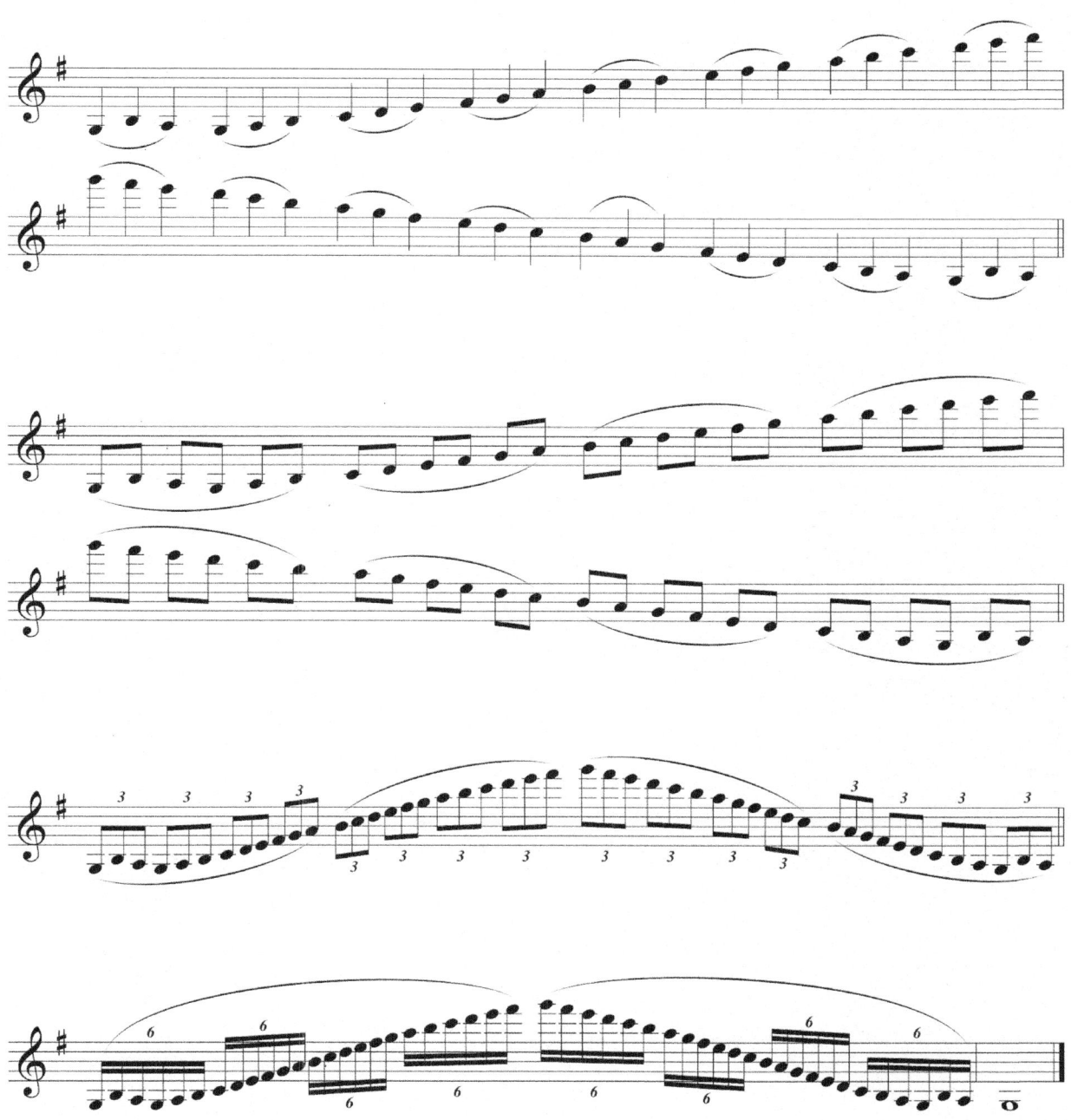

Rhythmic Accelerations
4 Octave Scales

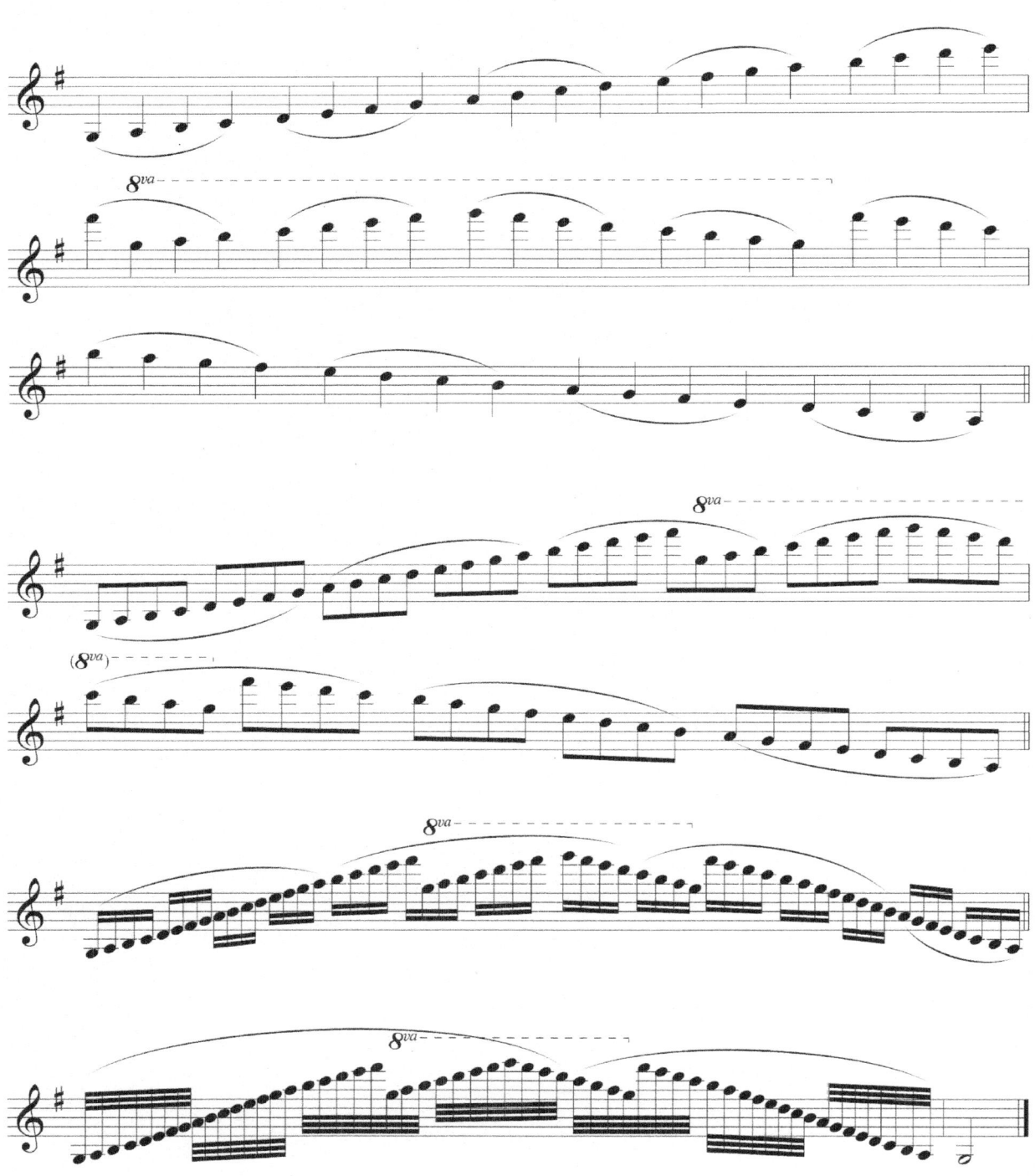

xxx

3 Octave Scales and Arpeggios

~~Fingers fo~~
- thumb + middle finger touch @ metal

G Major / G Minor

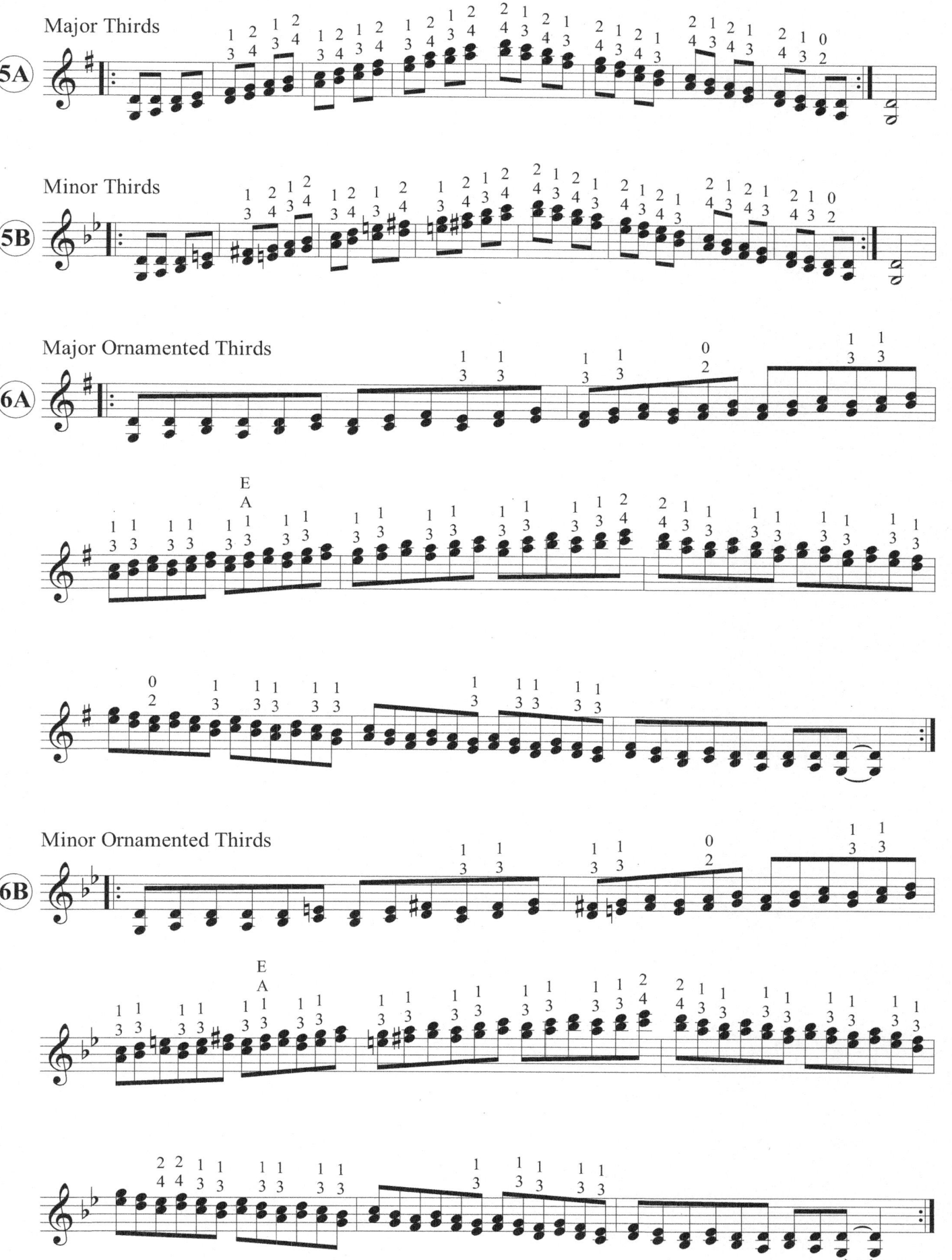

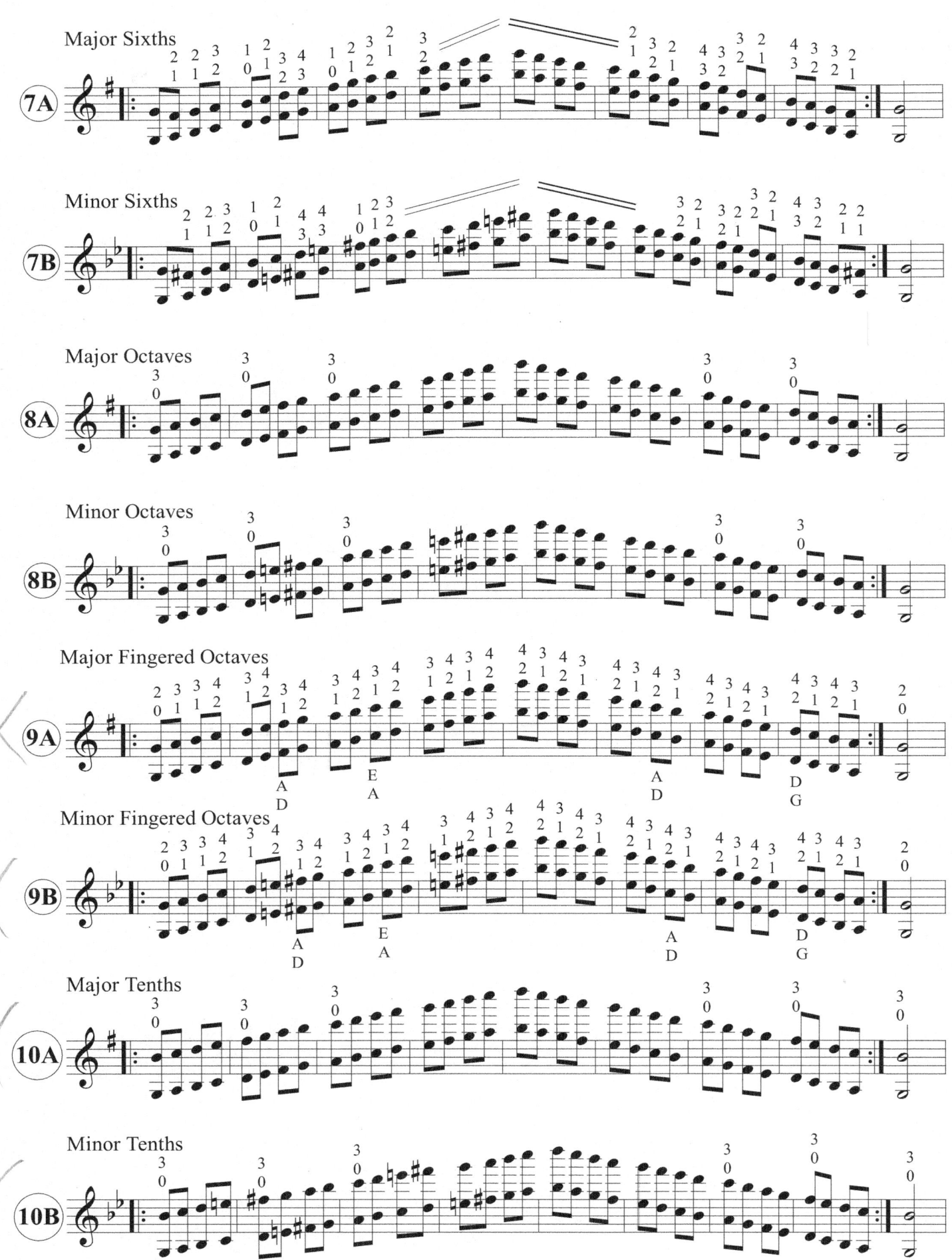

A♭ Major / A♭ Minor

Major Scale

1A

Minor Scale

1B

Major Ornamented Scale

2A

Minor Ornamented Scale

2B

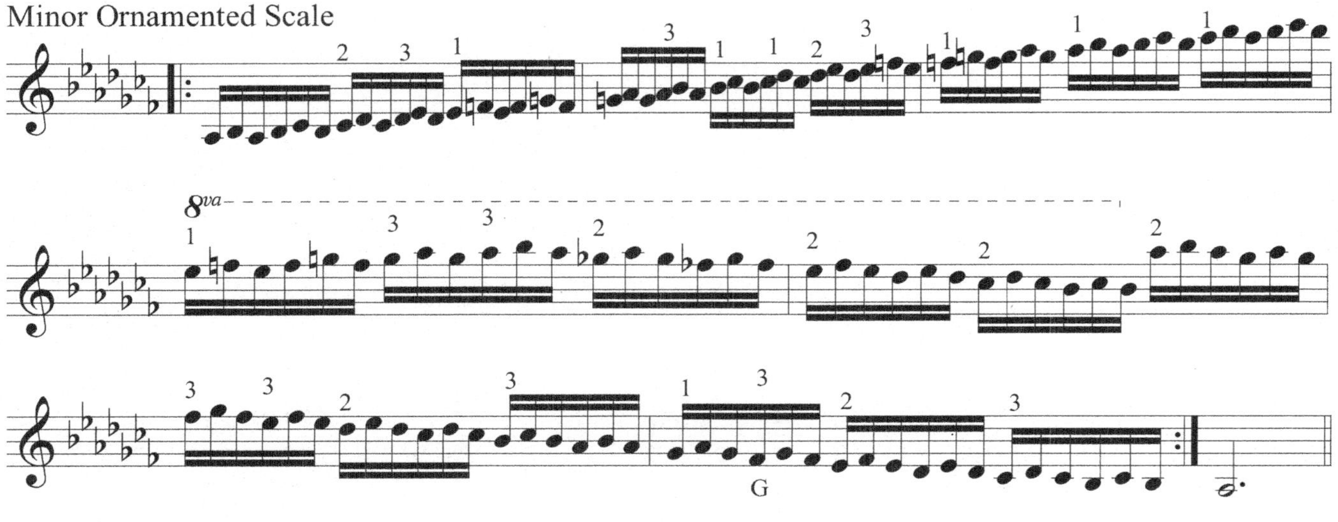

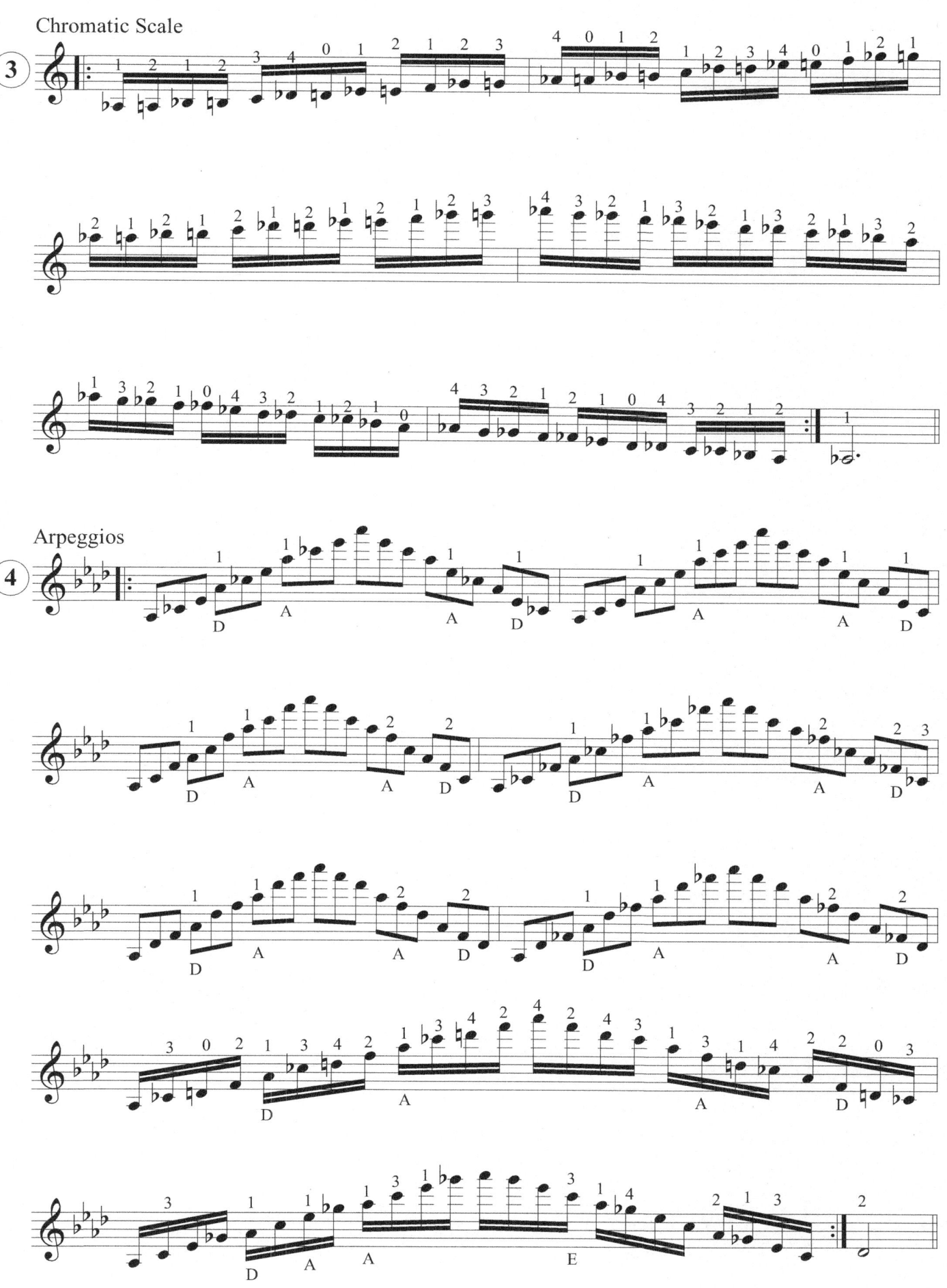

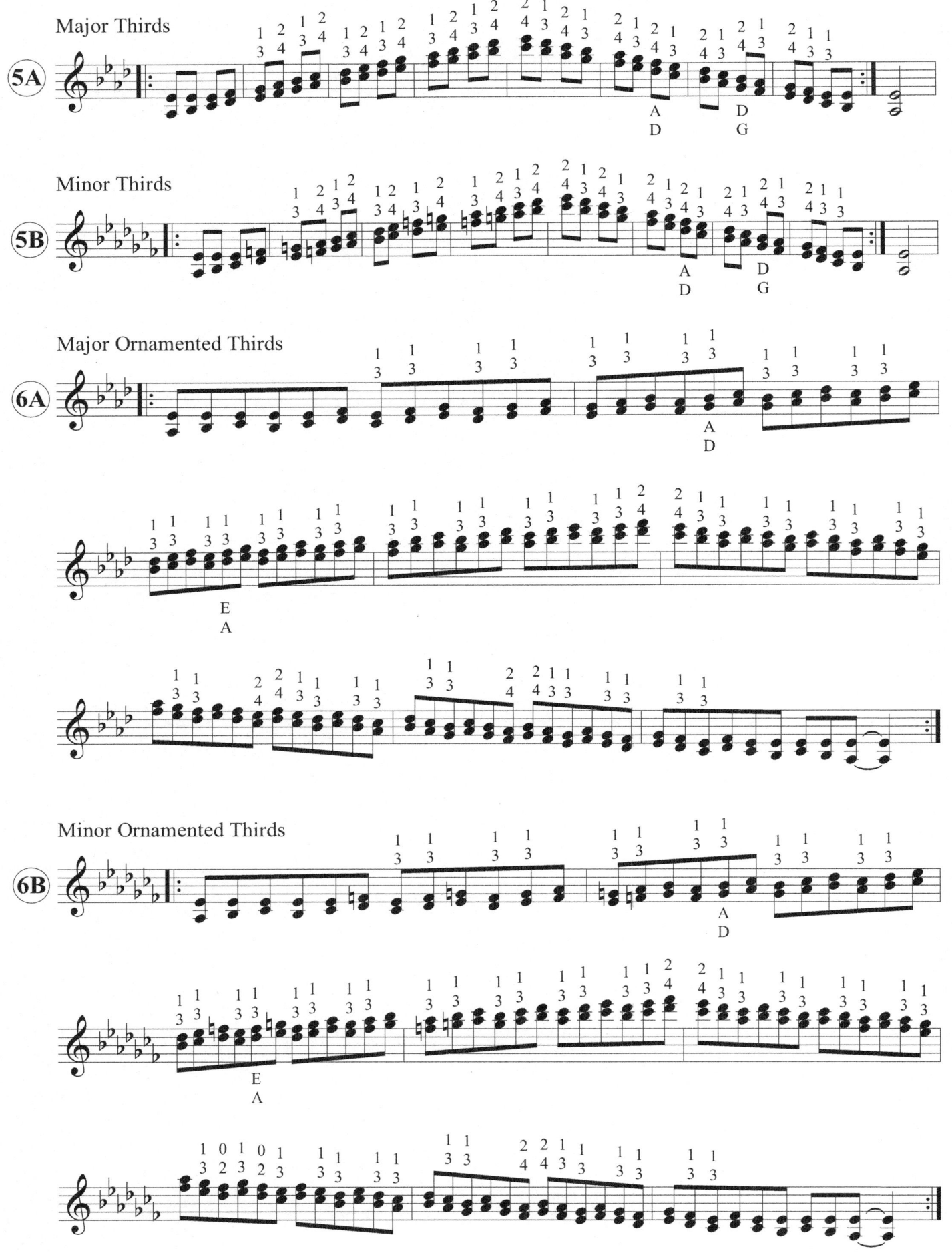

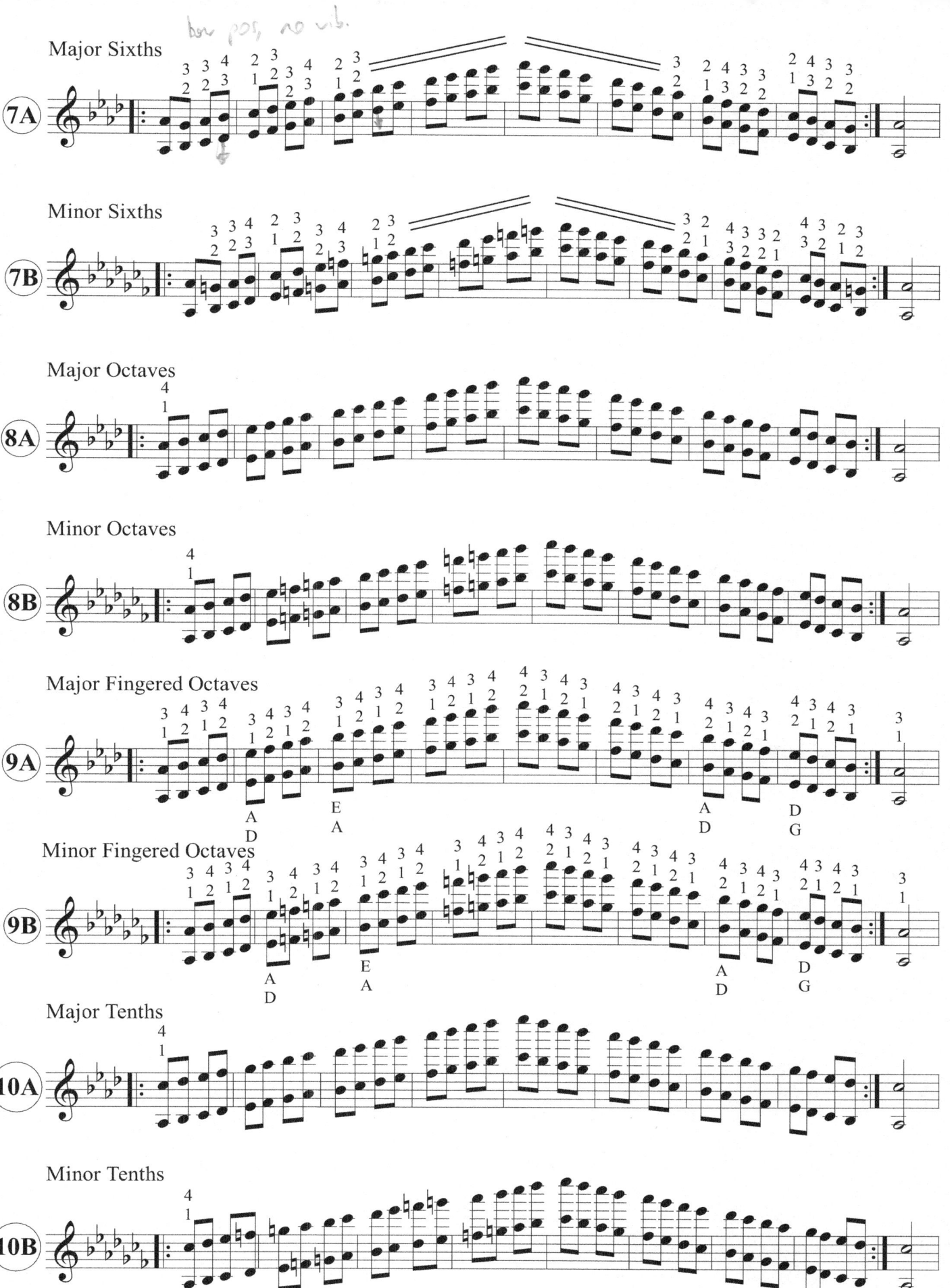

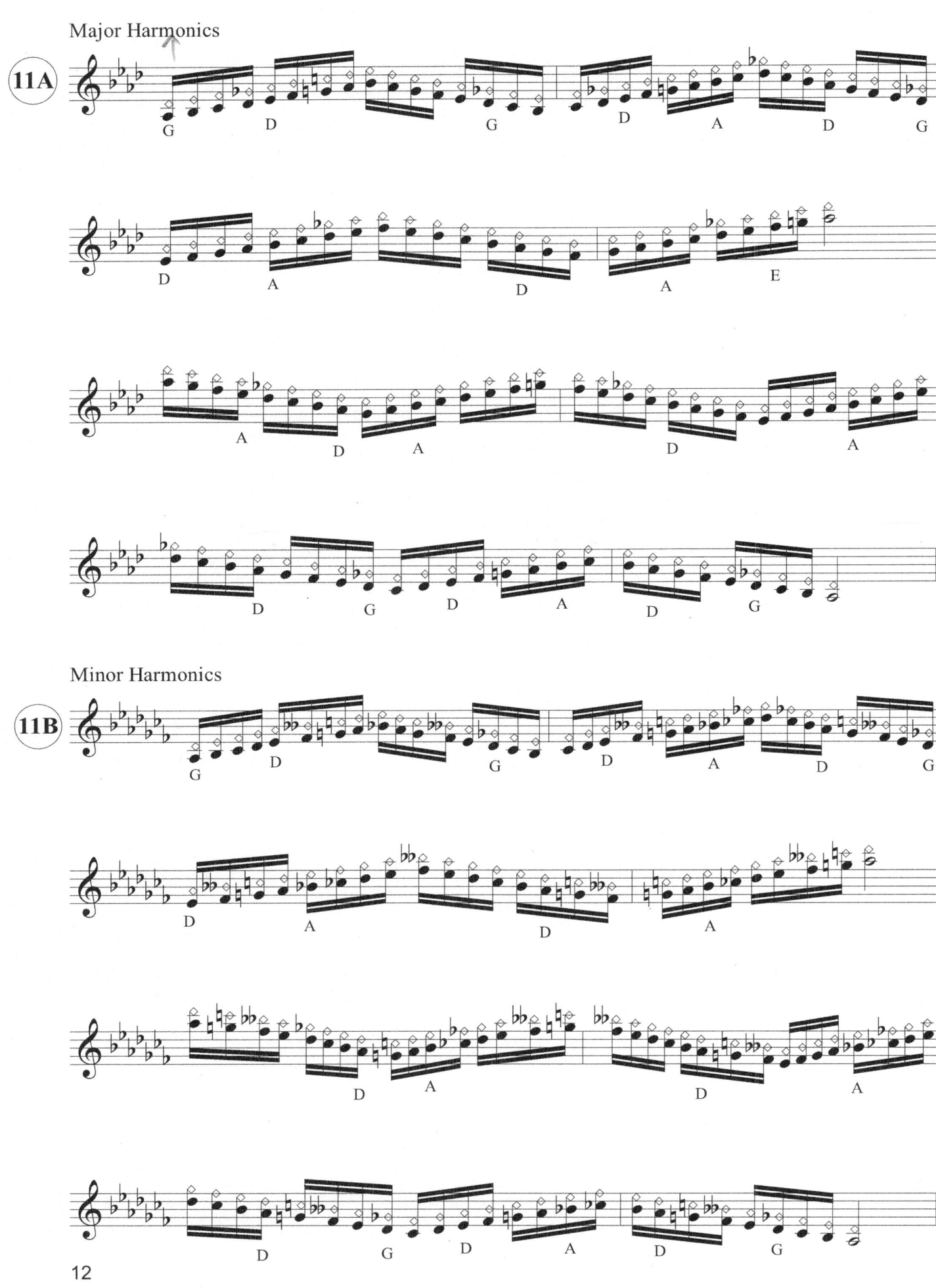

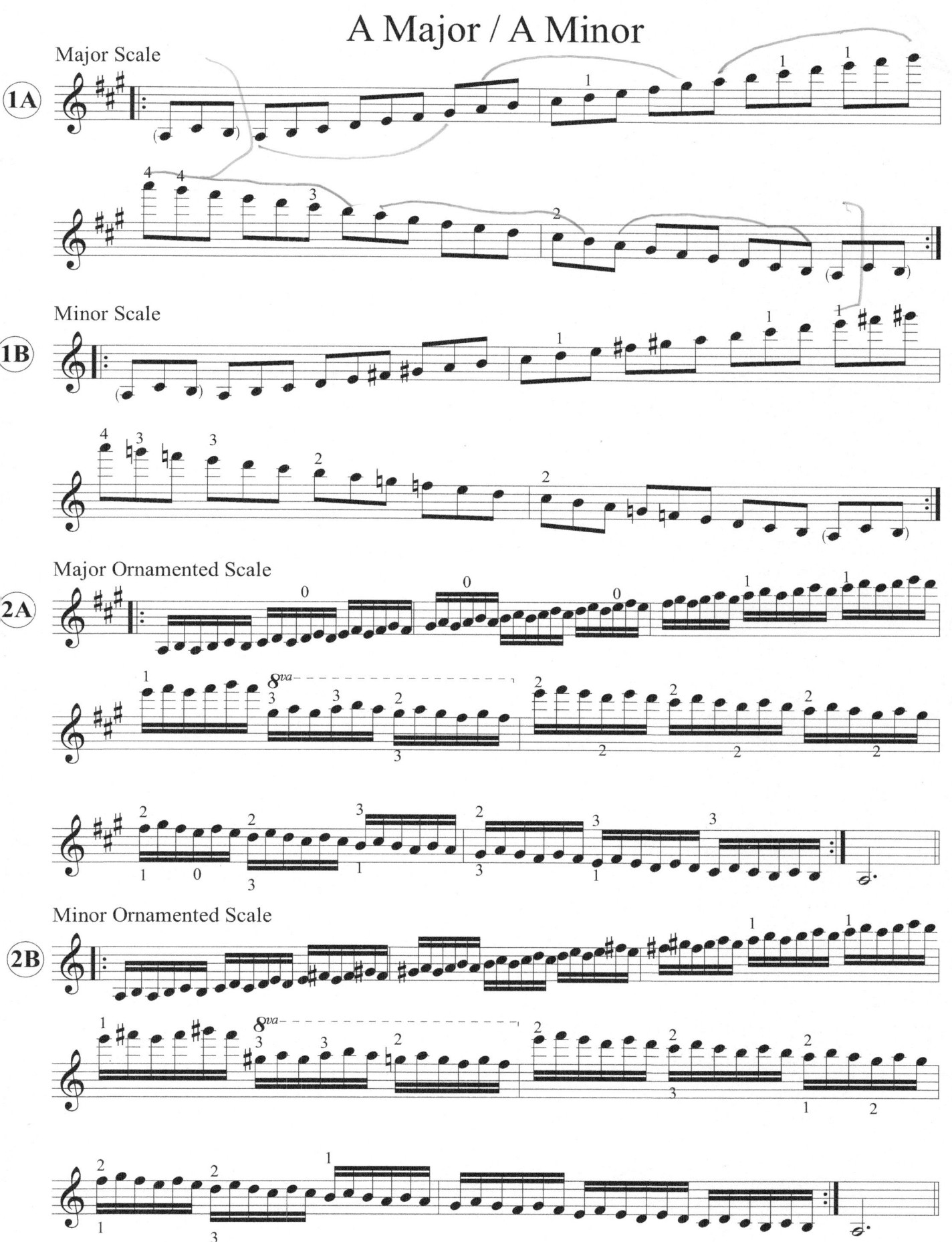

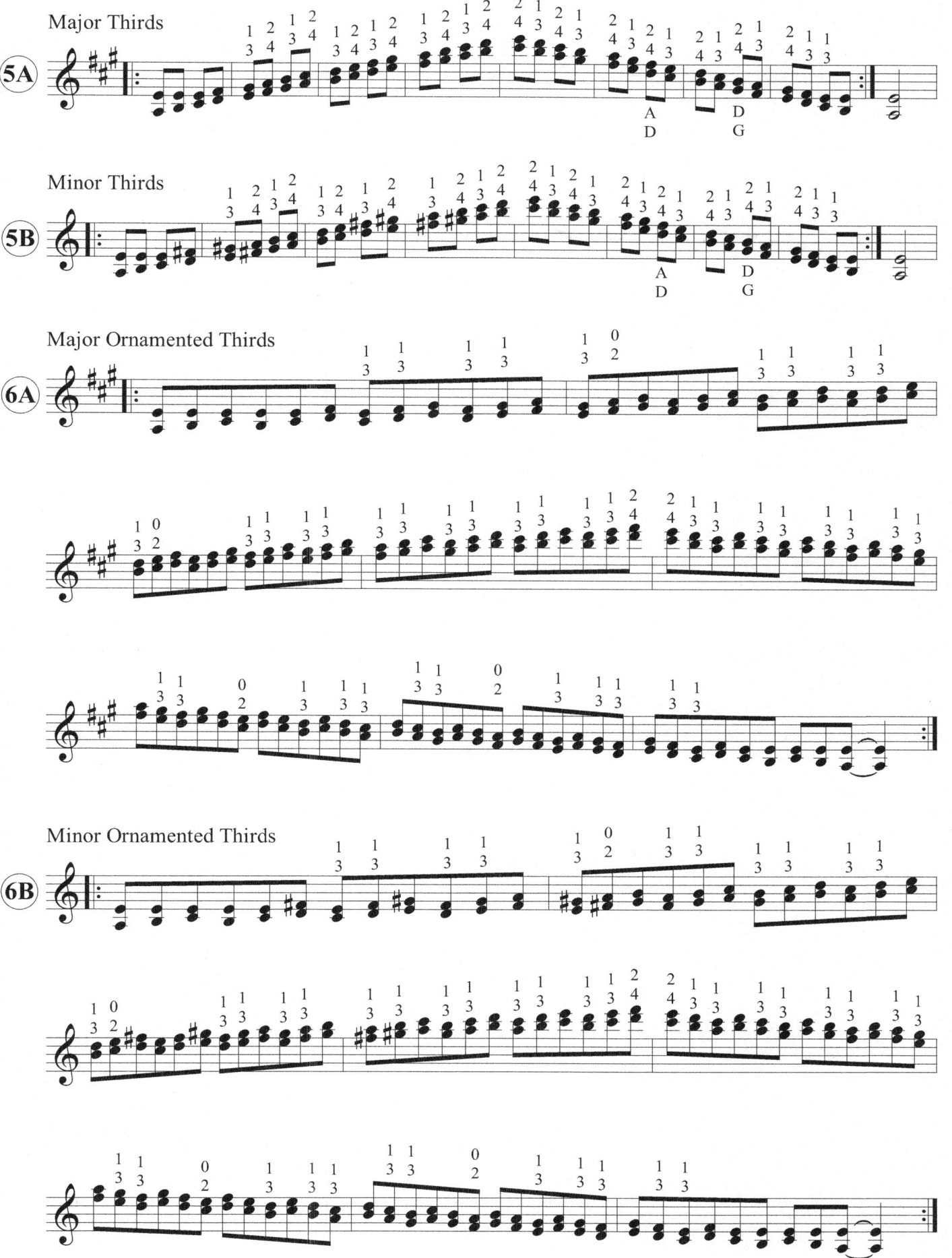

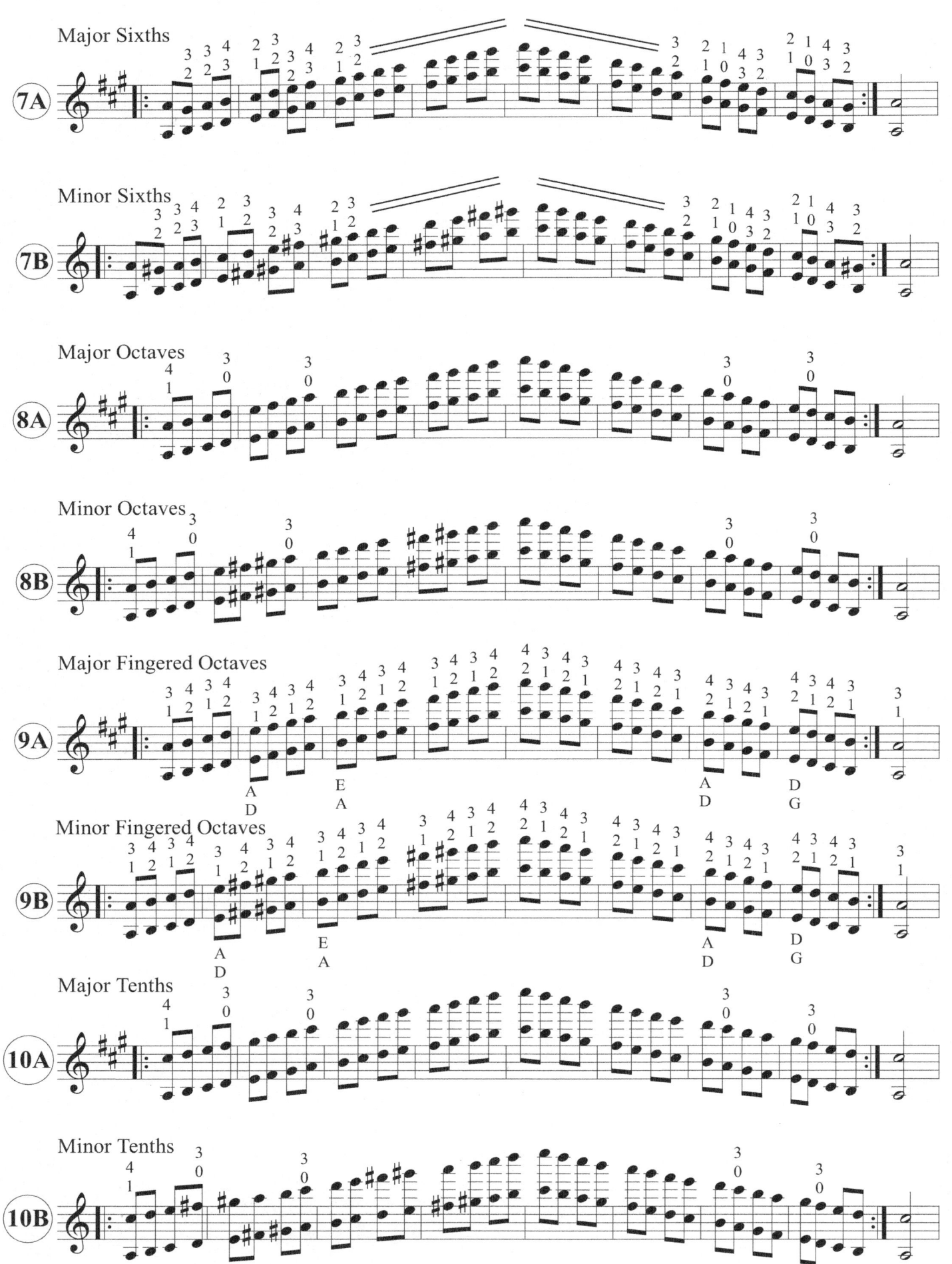

Major Harmonics

Minor Harmonics

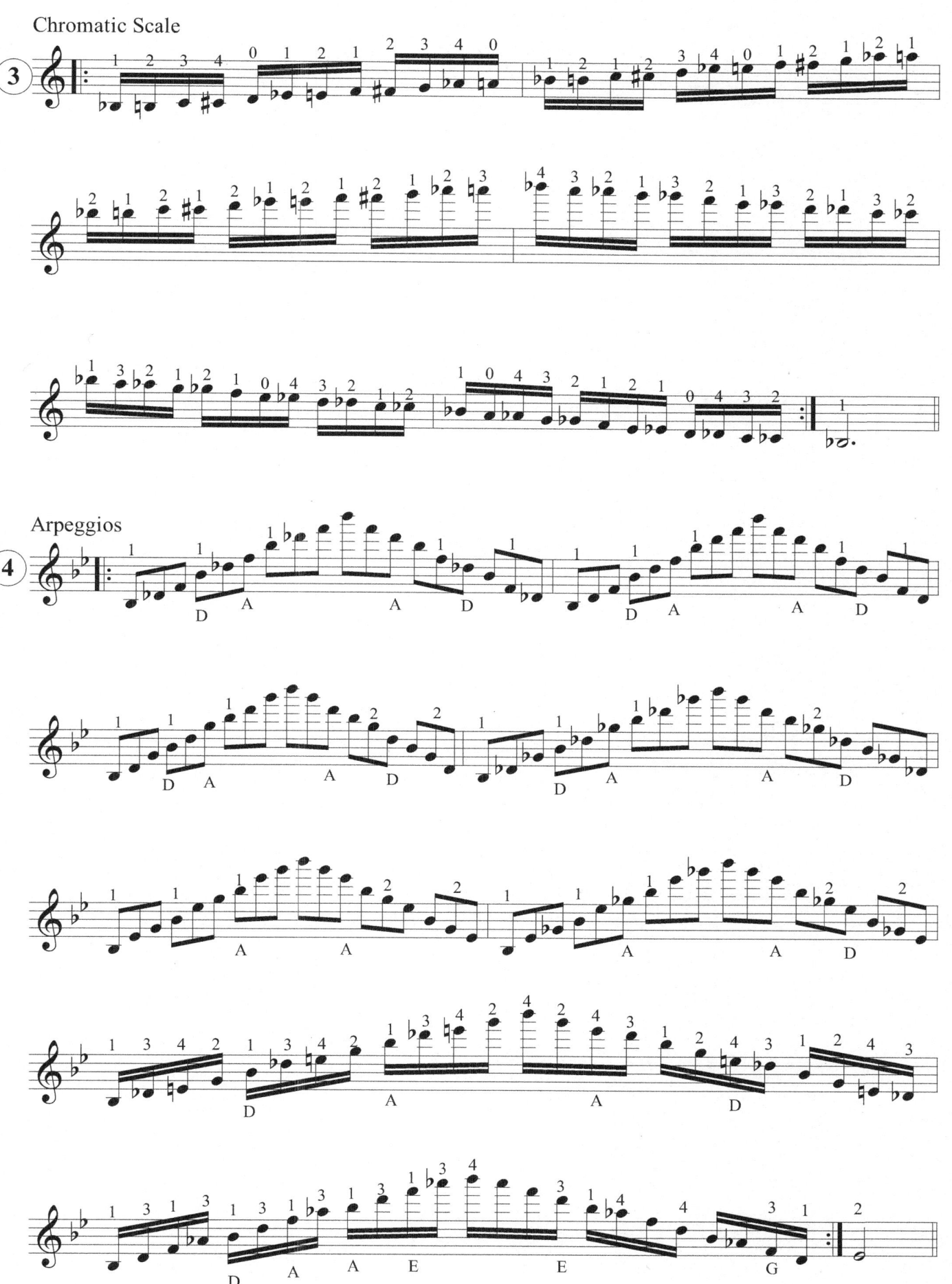

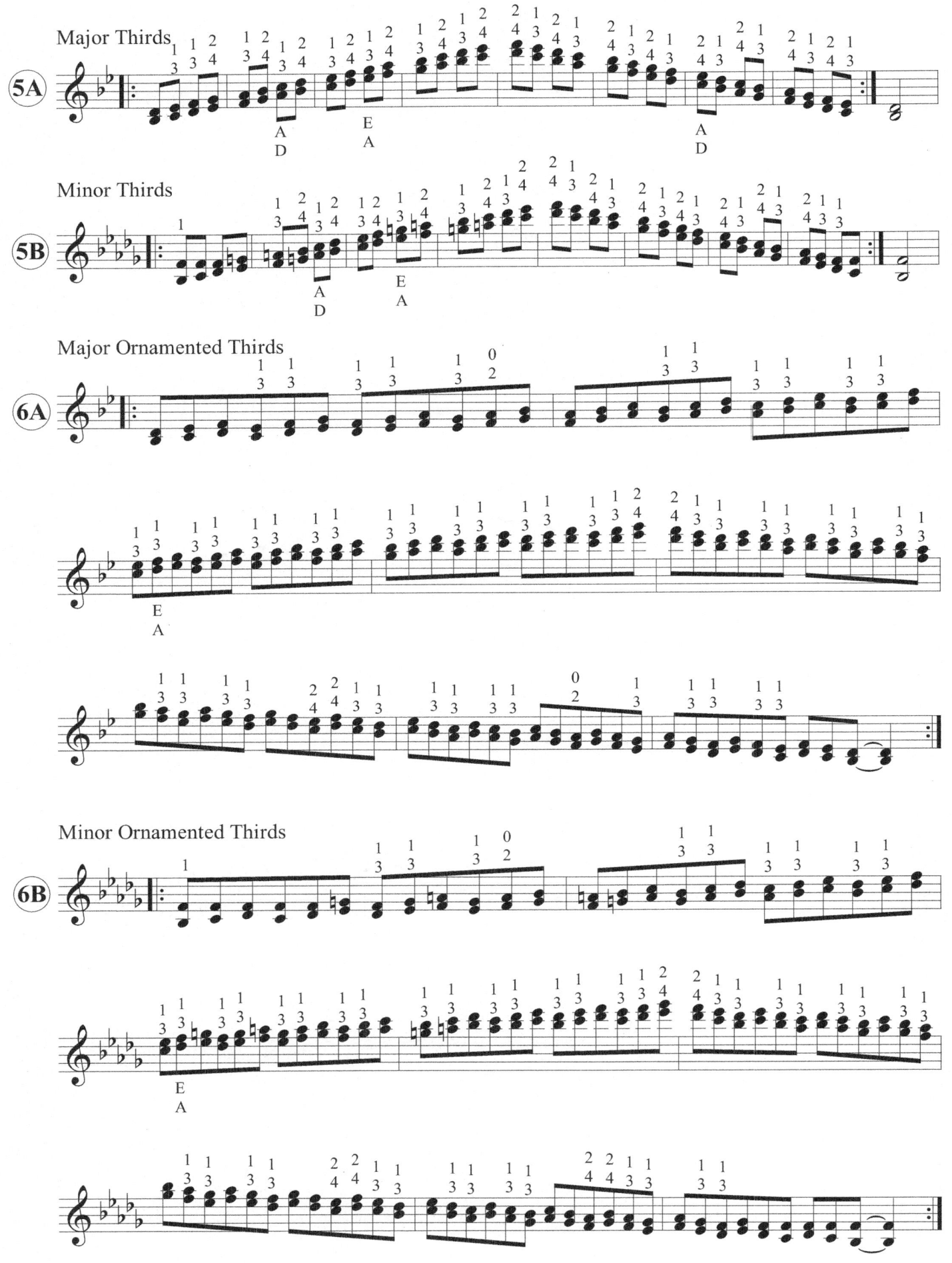

Major Harmonics

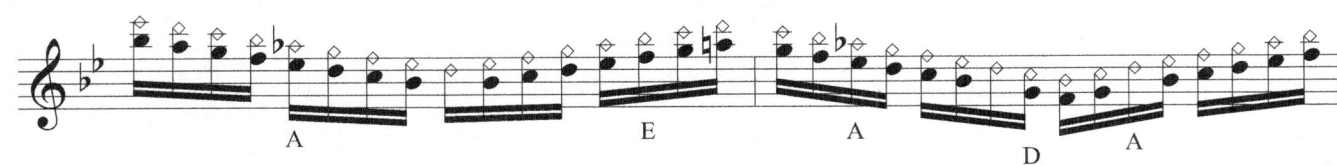

Minor Harmonics

22

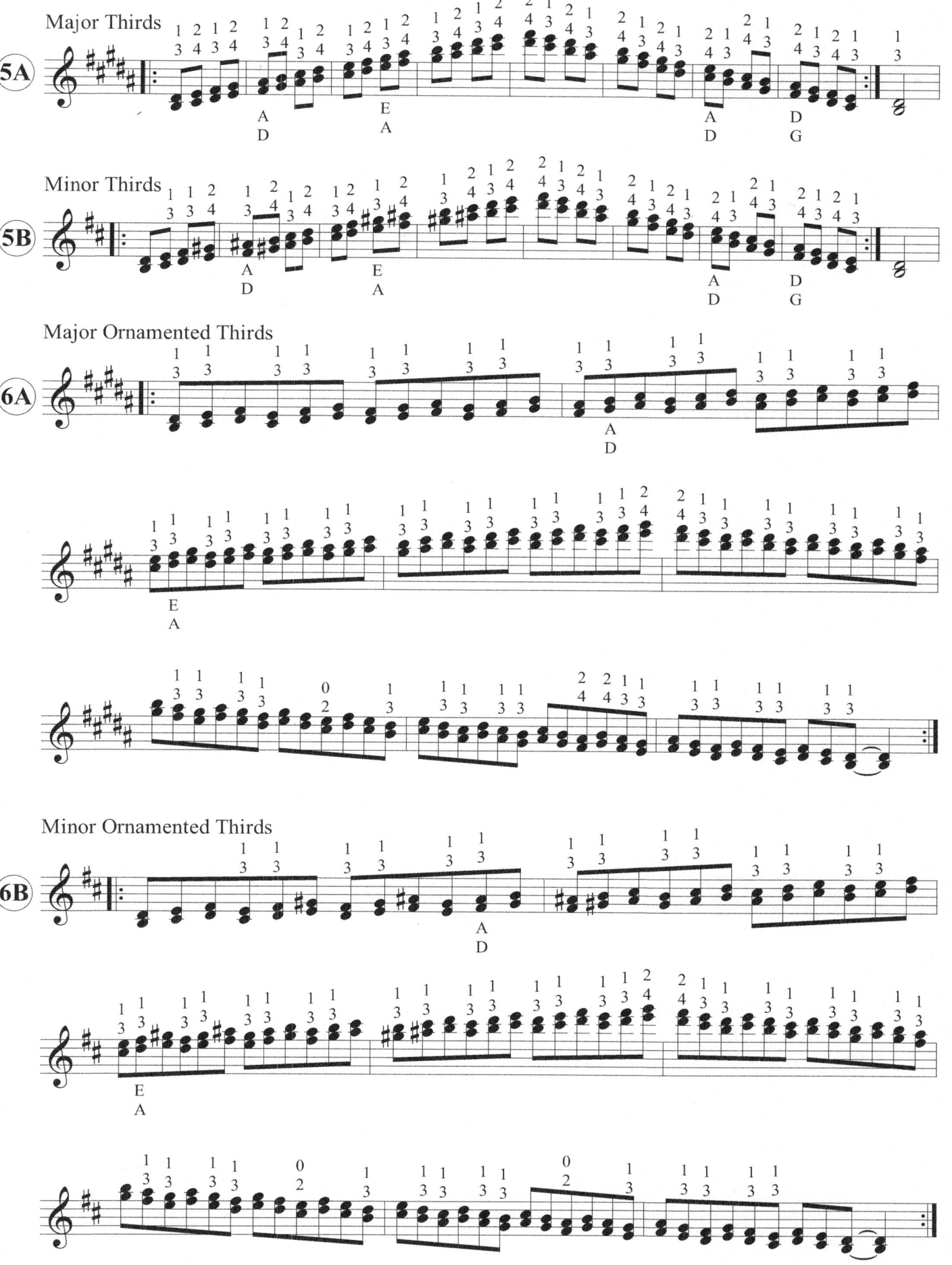

Major Harmonics

Minor Harmonics

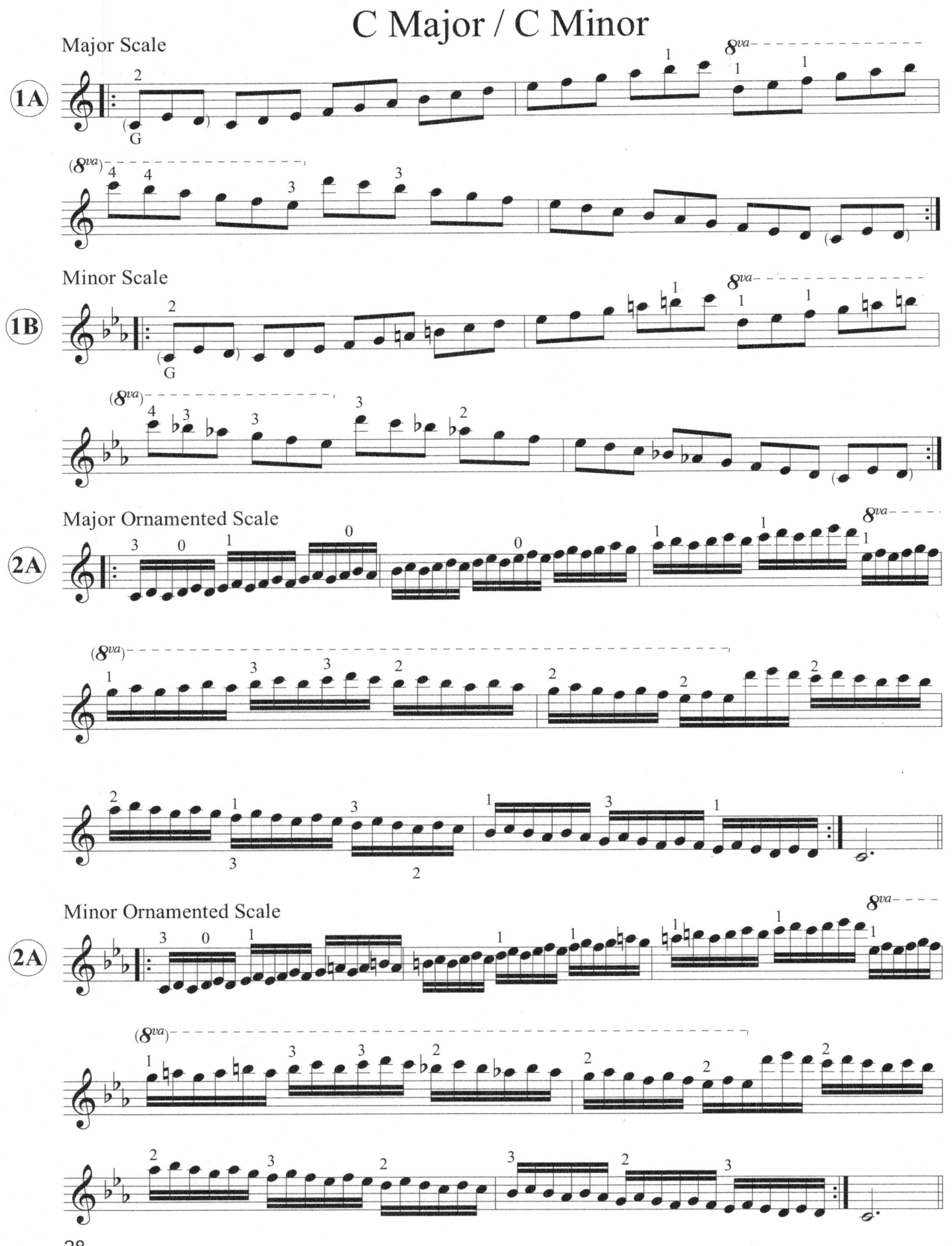

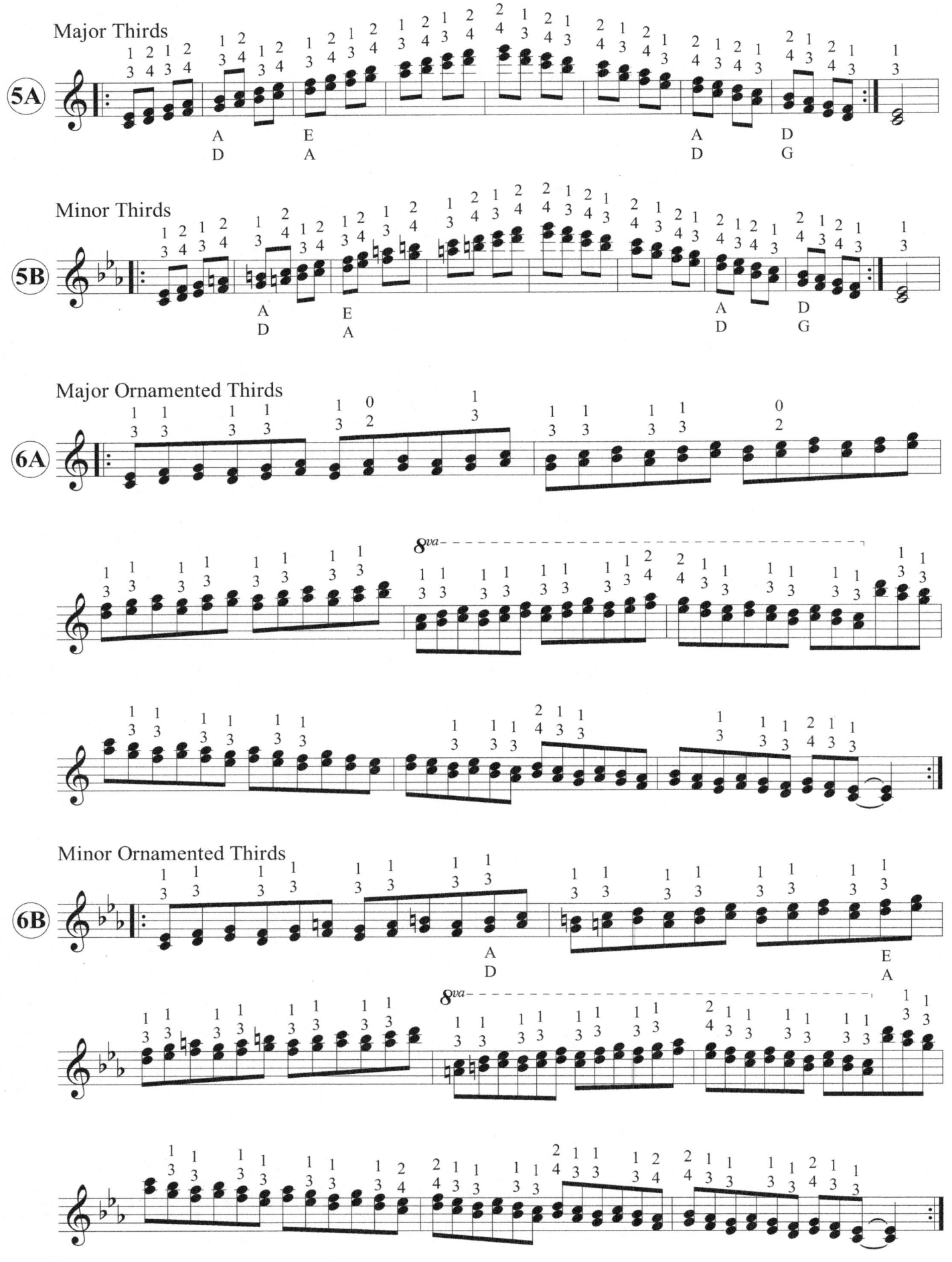

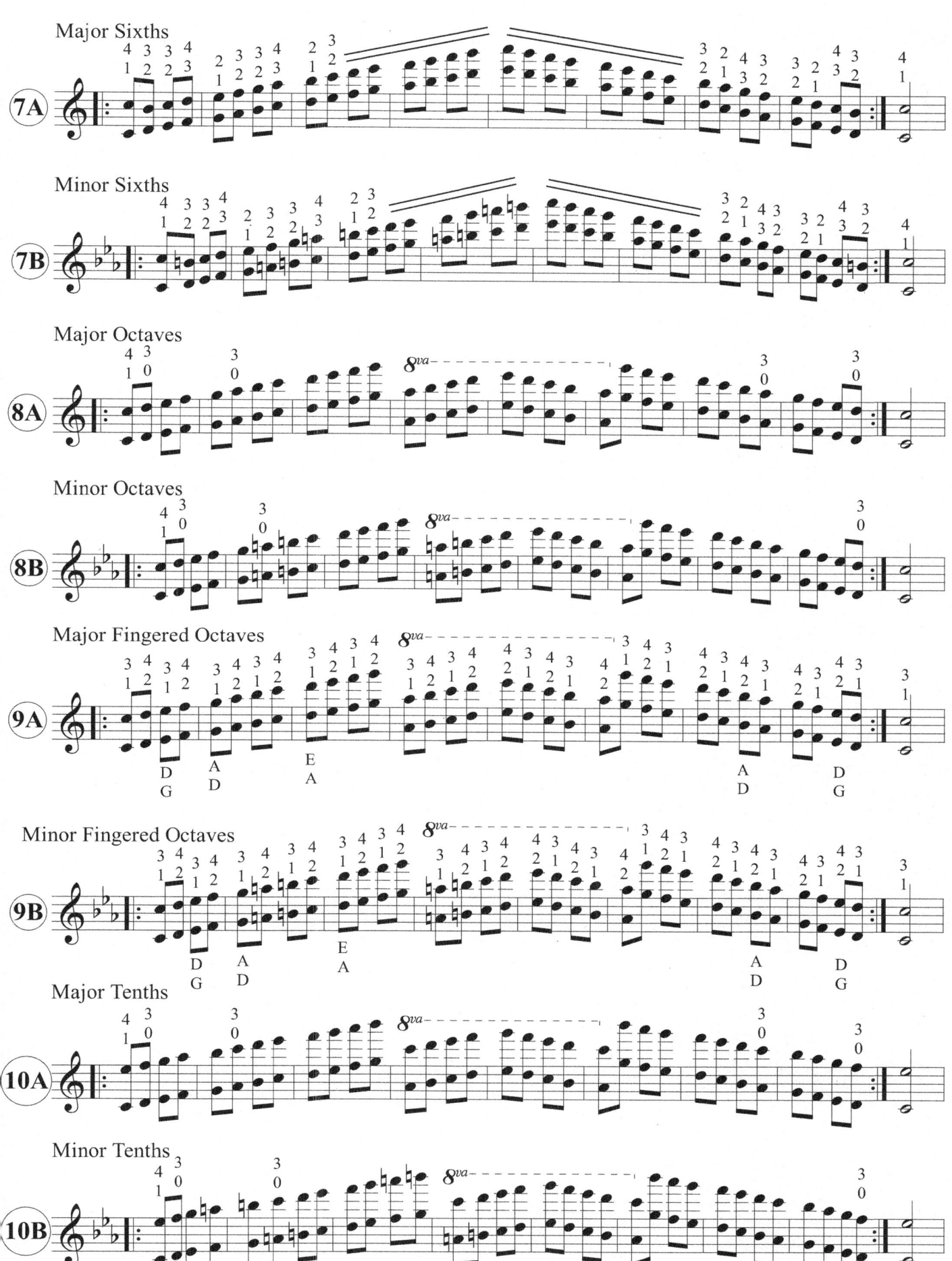

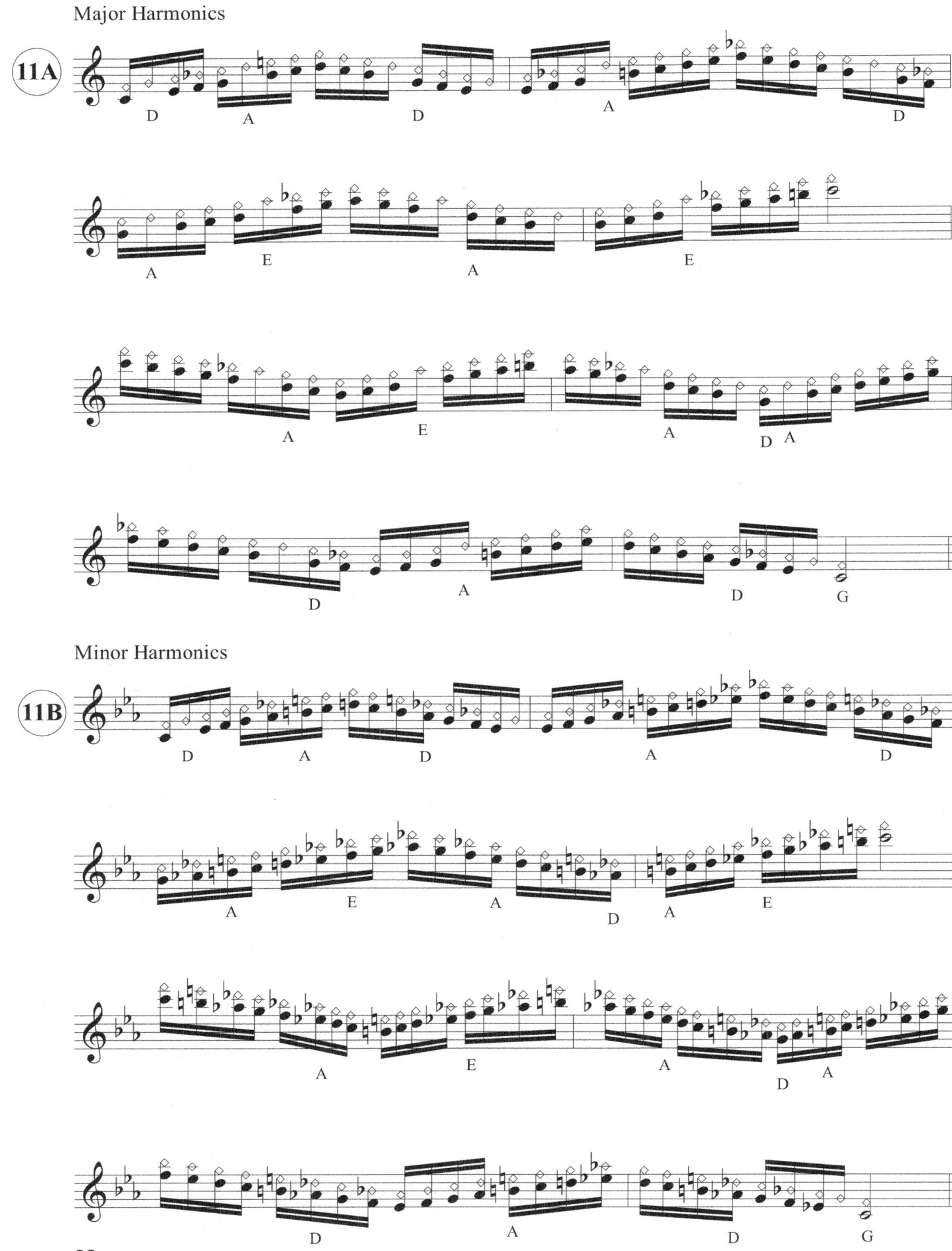

Chromatic Scale

Arpeggios

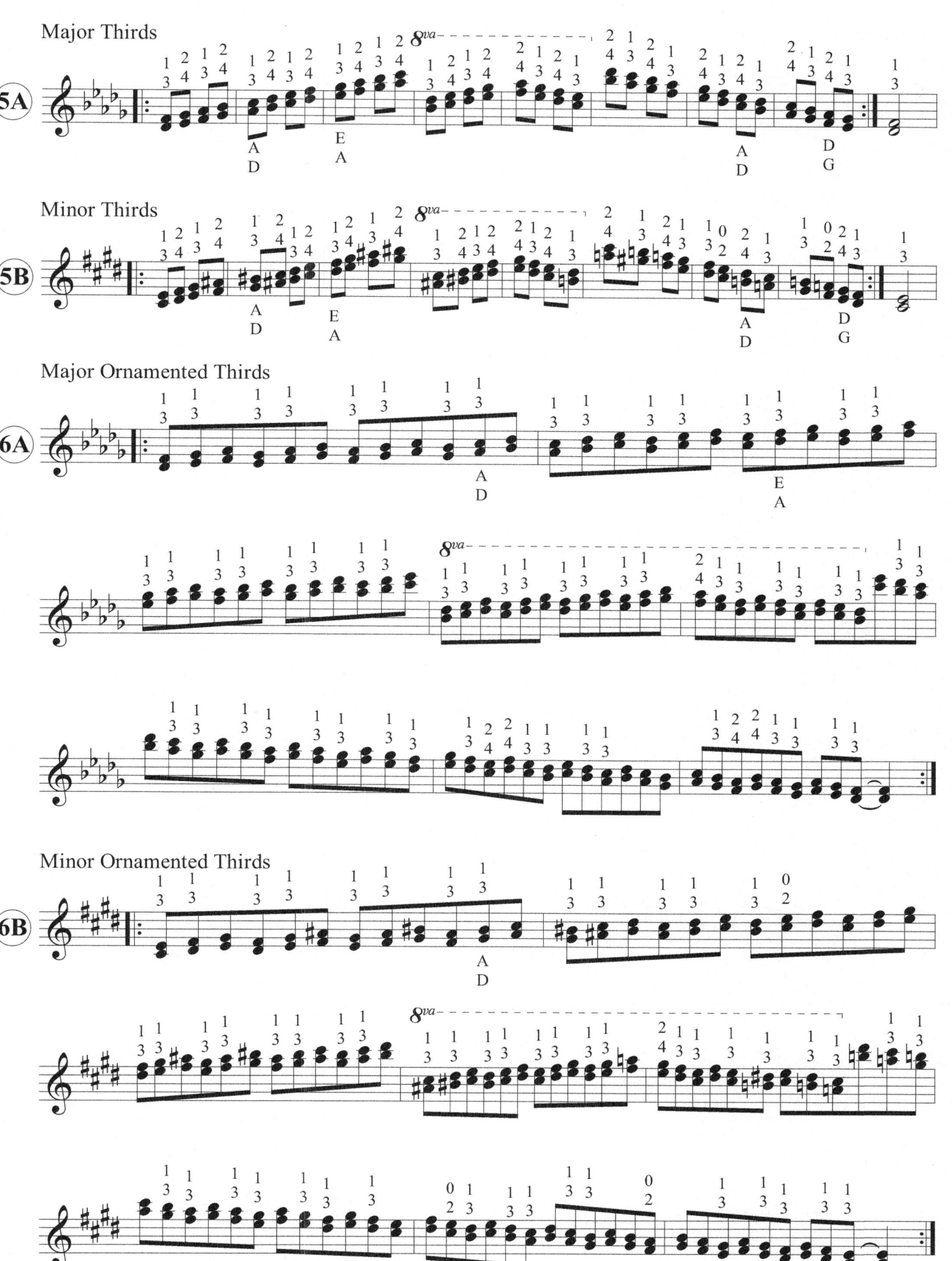

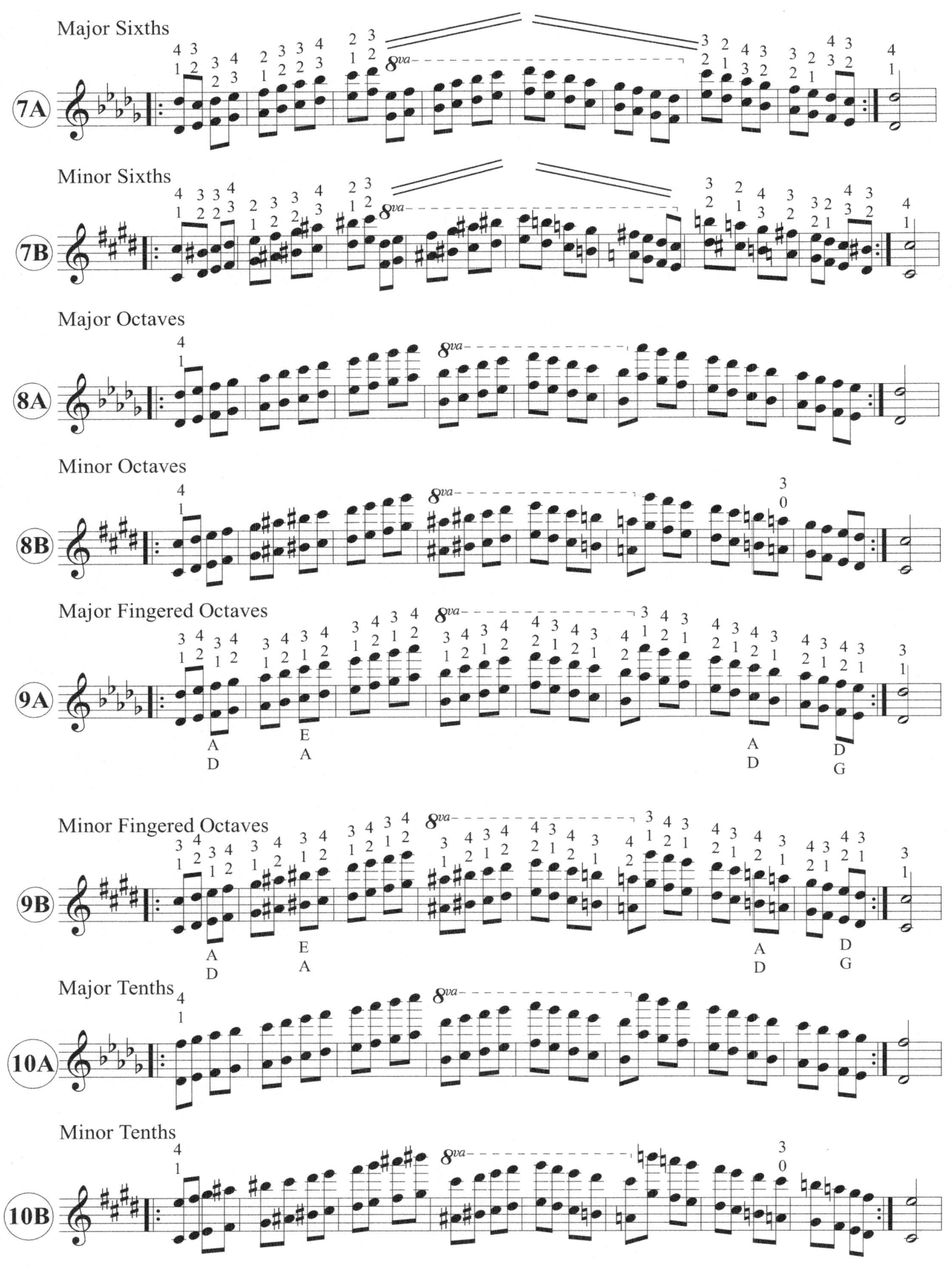

Major Harmonics

Minor Harmonics

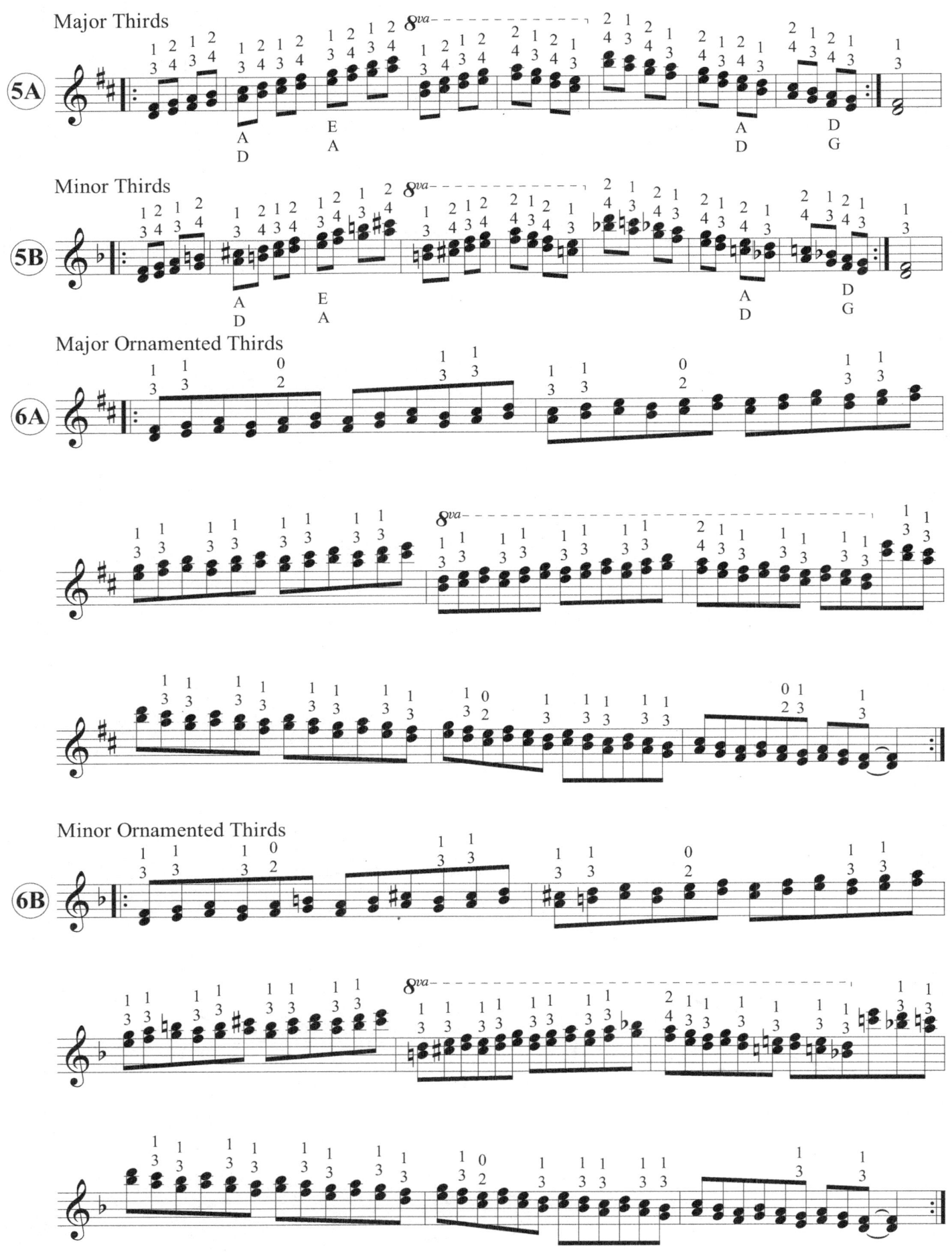

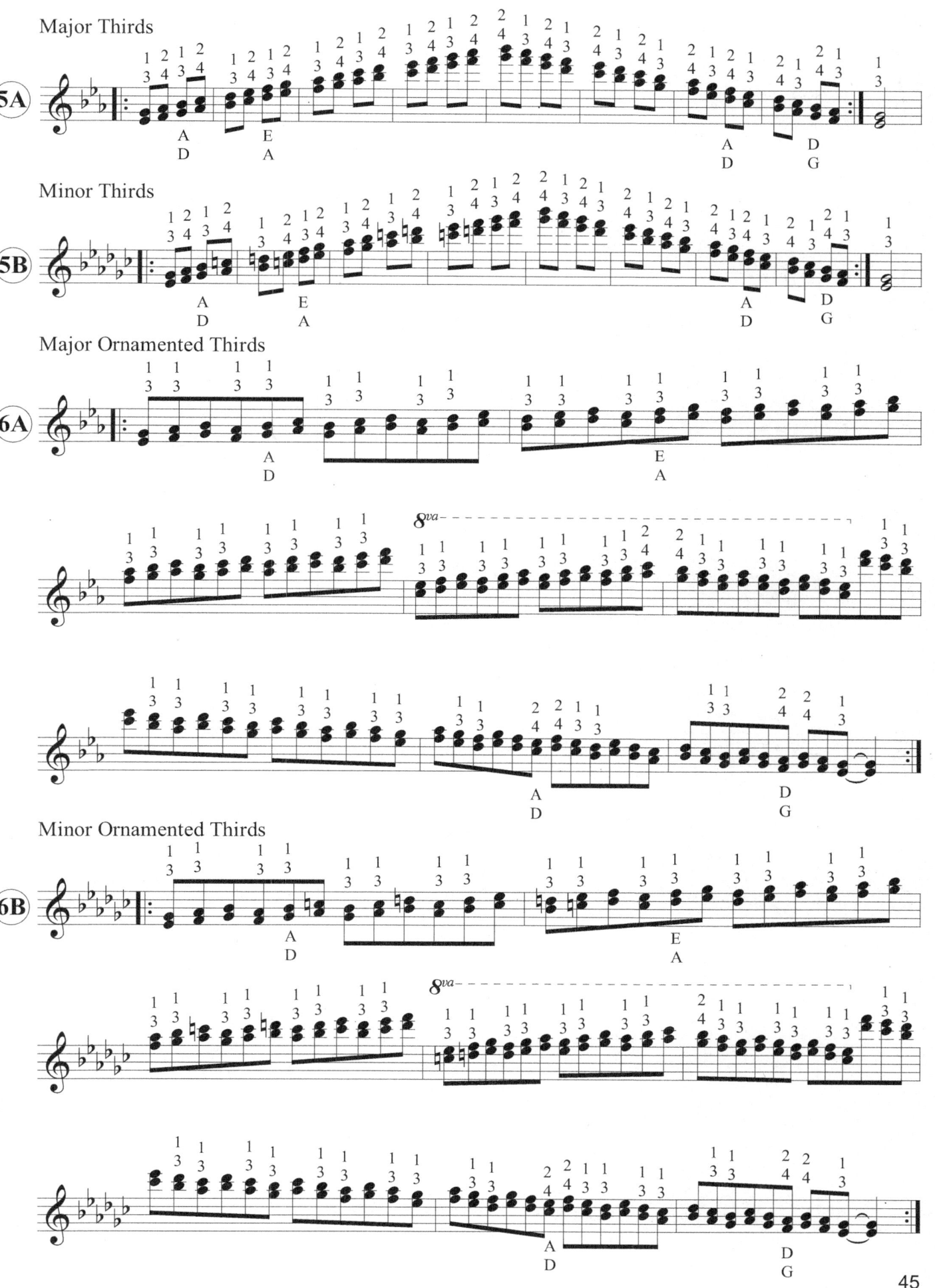

Major Harmonics

Minor Harmonics

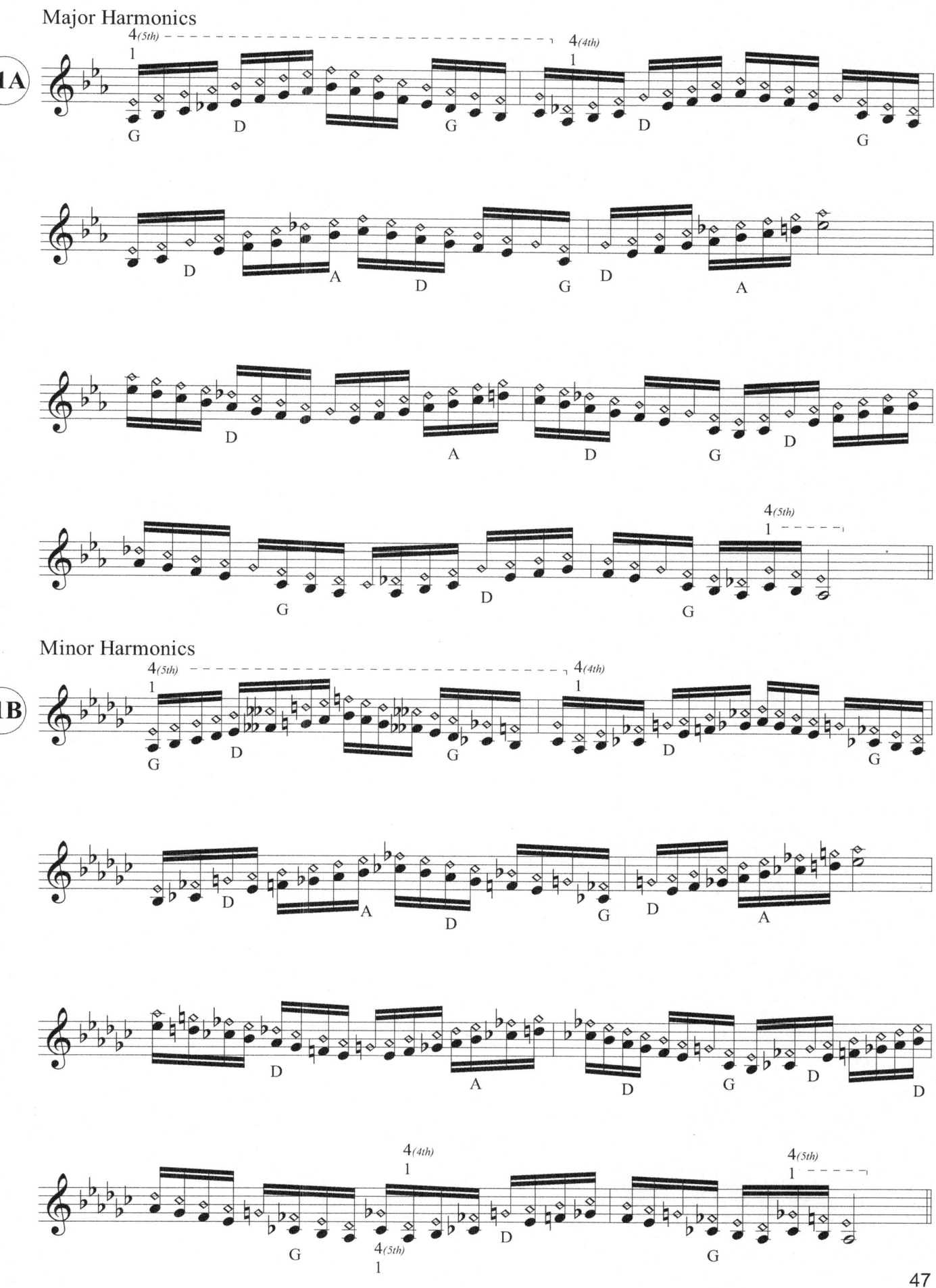

E Major / E Minor

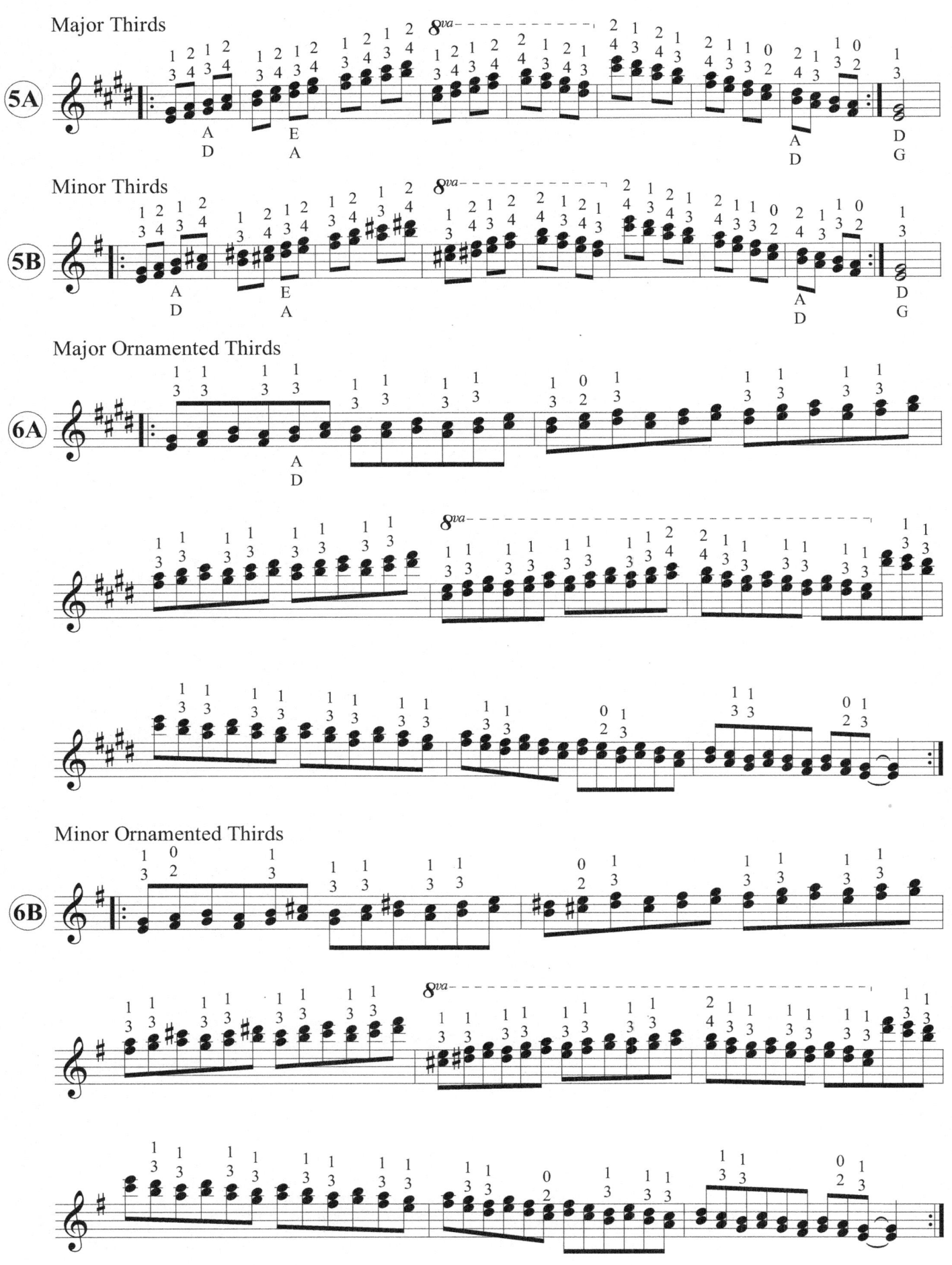

F Major / F Minor

Chromatic Scale

Arpeggios

54

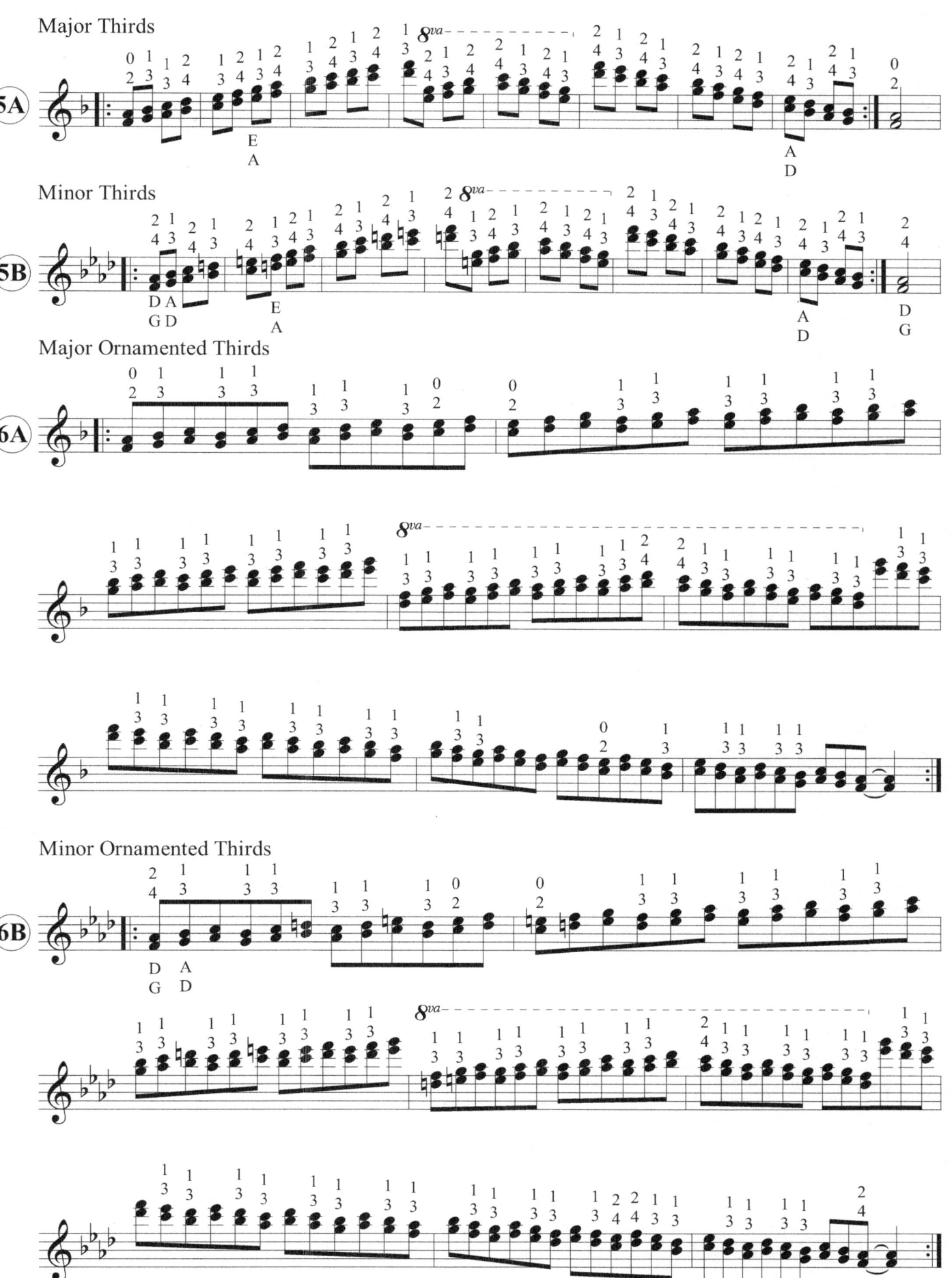

Major Harmonics

Minor Harmonics

F# Major / F# Minor

Chromatic Scale

Arpeggios

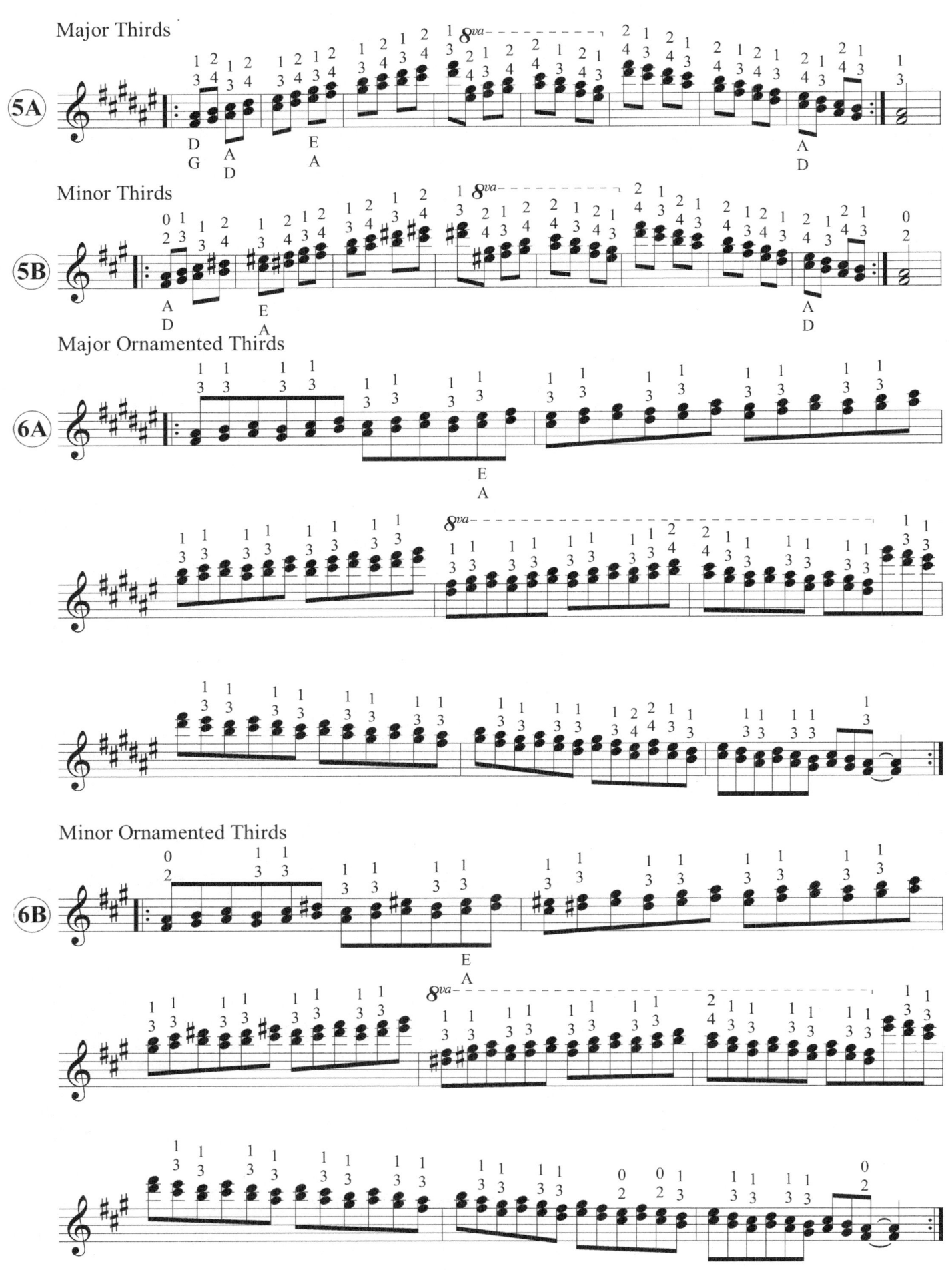

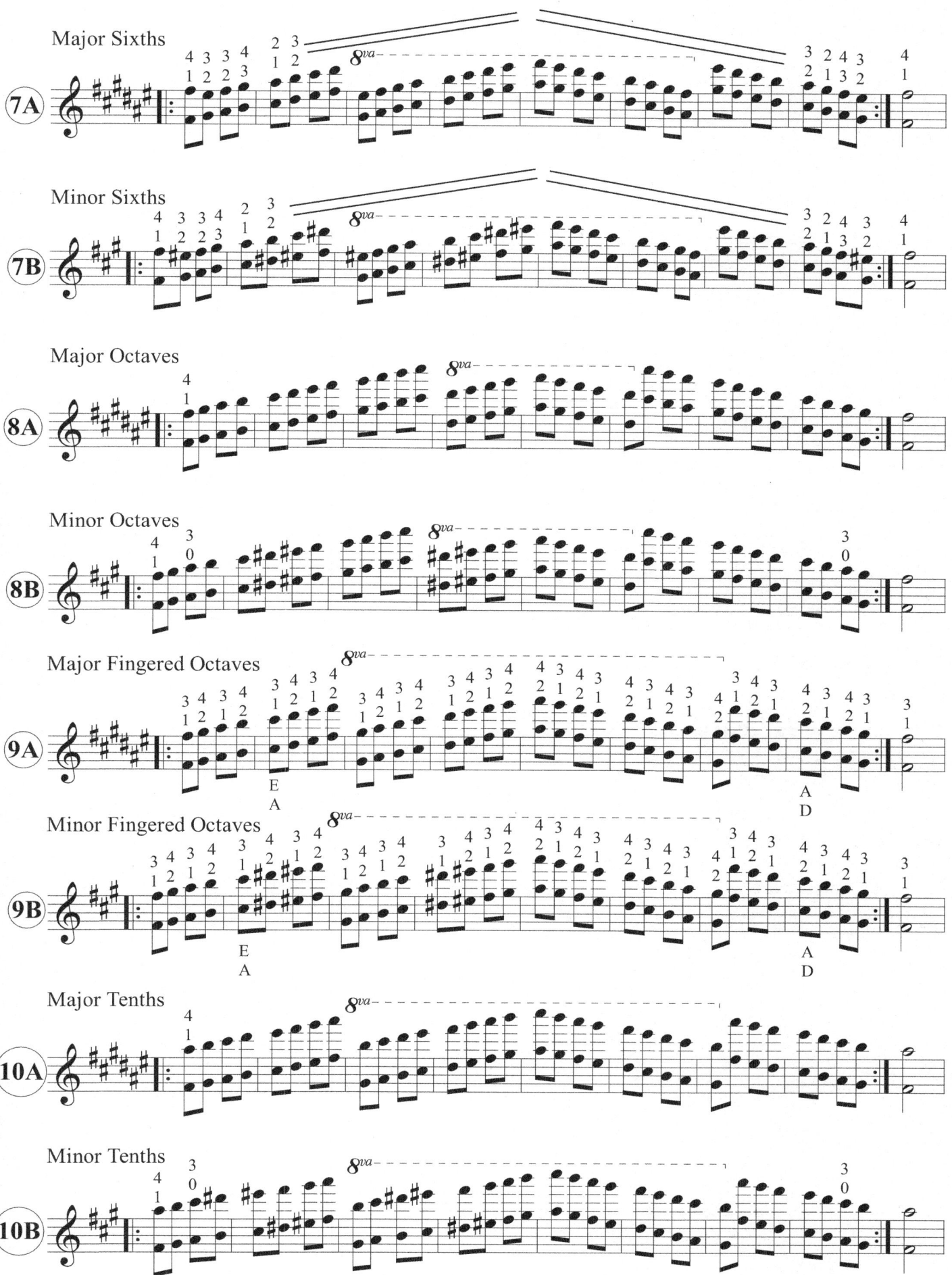

4 Octave Scales and Arpeggios

G Major / G Minor

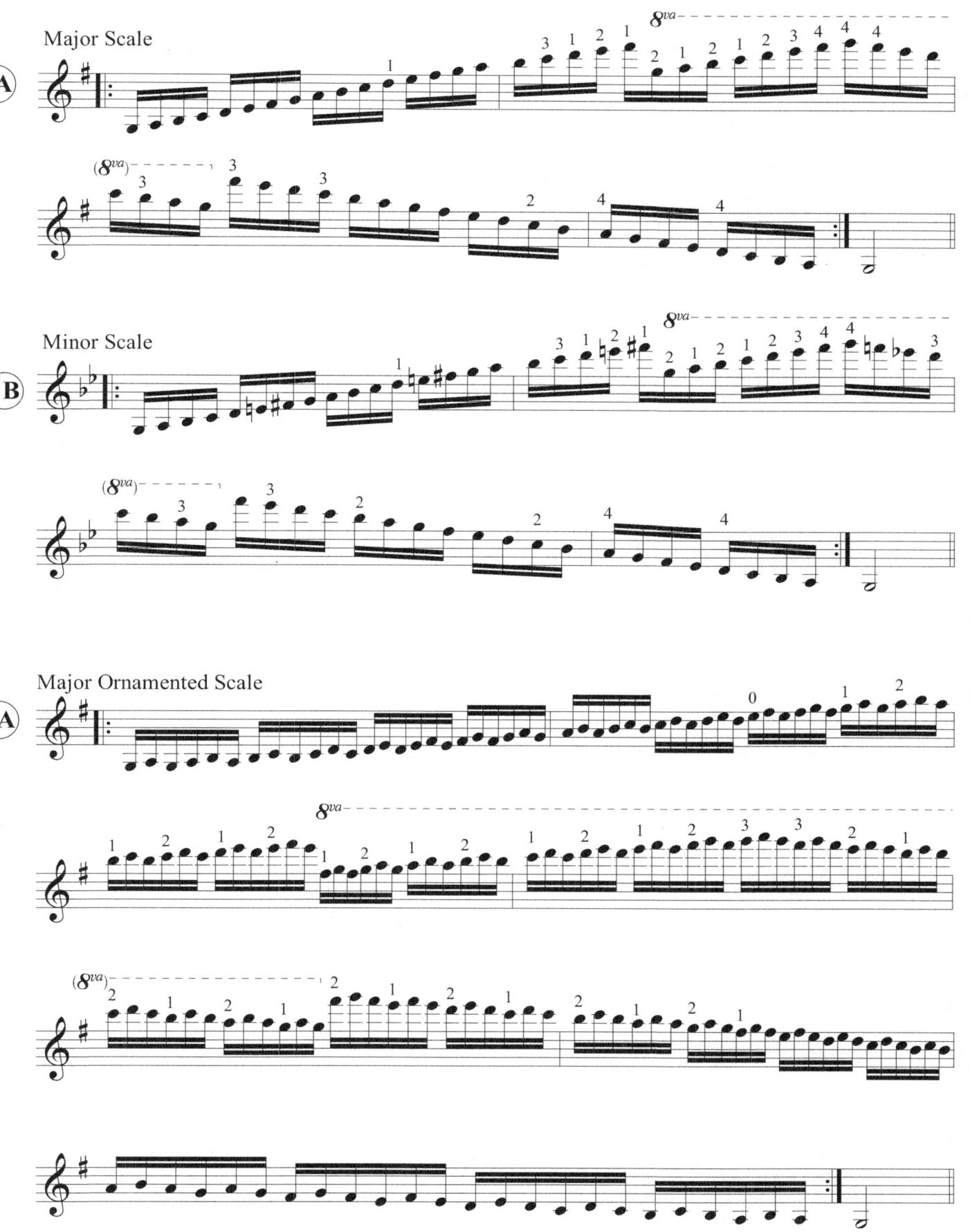

Minor Ornamented Scale

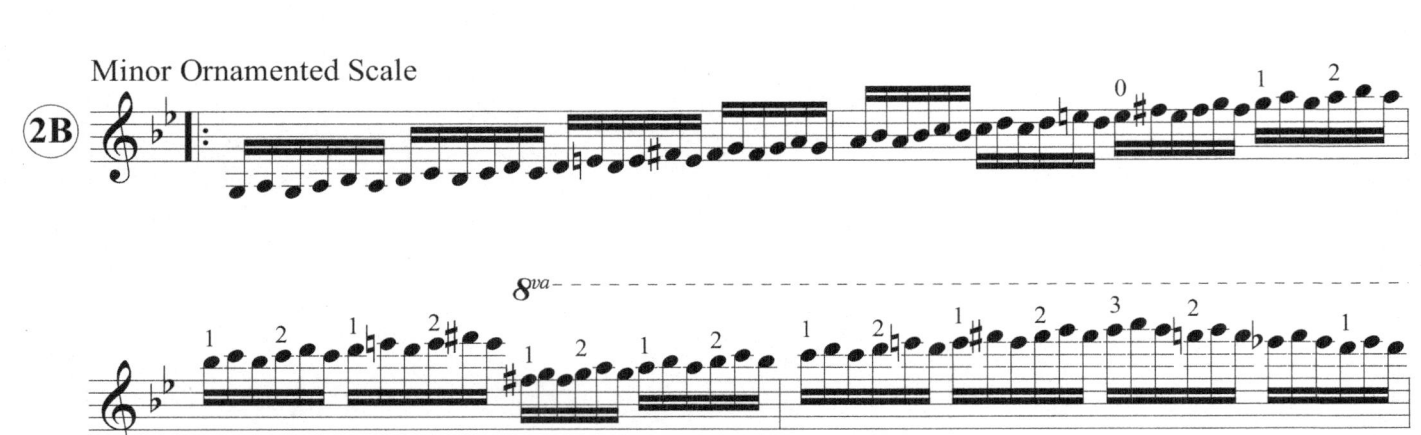

Chromatic Scale

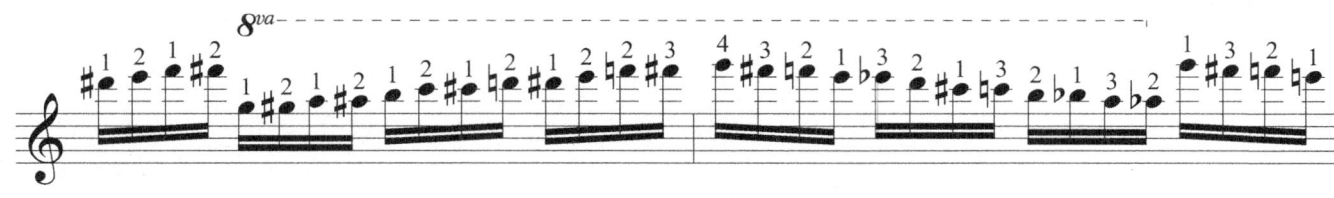

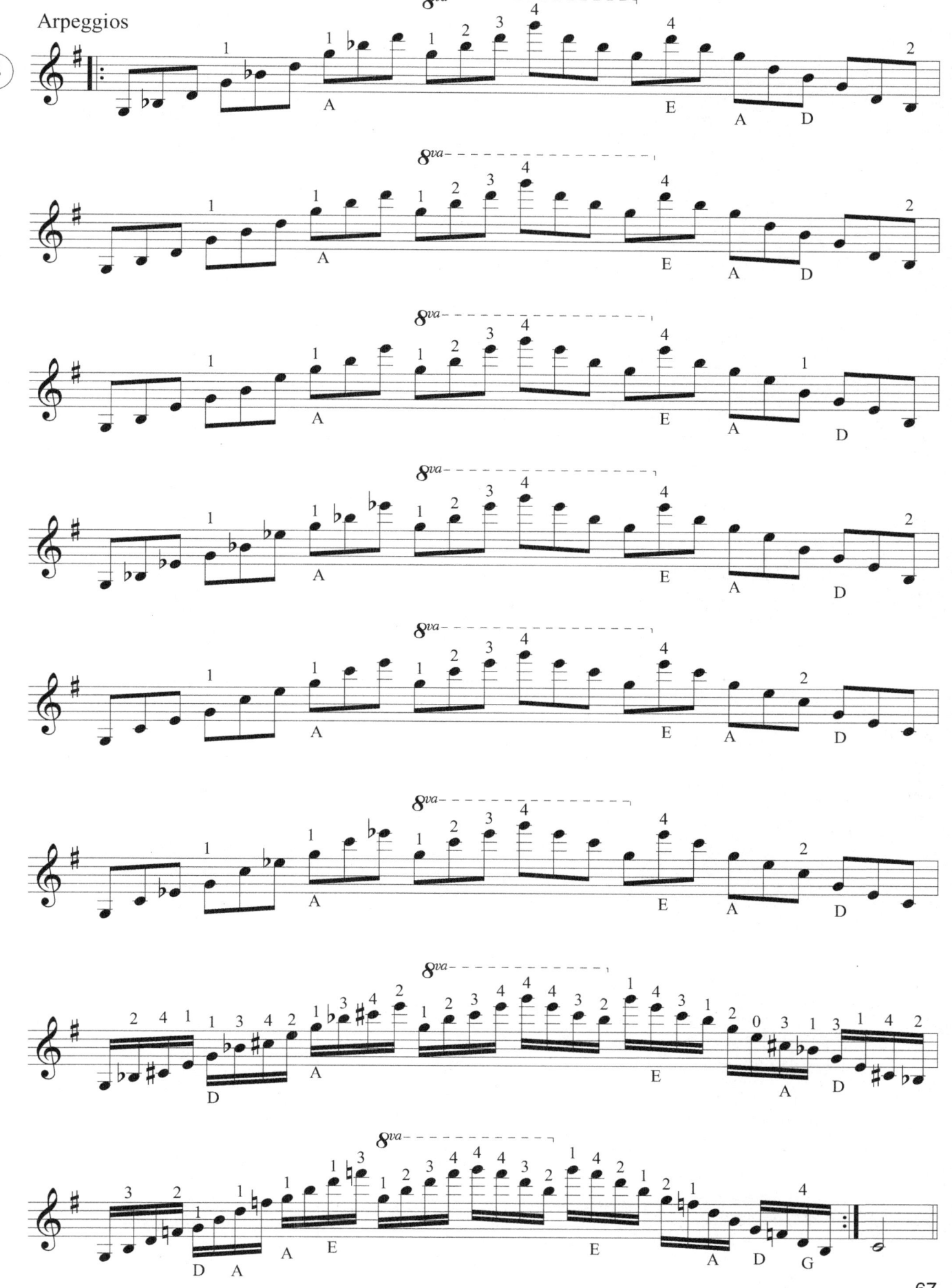

Ab Major / Ab Minor

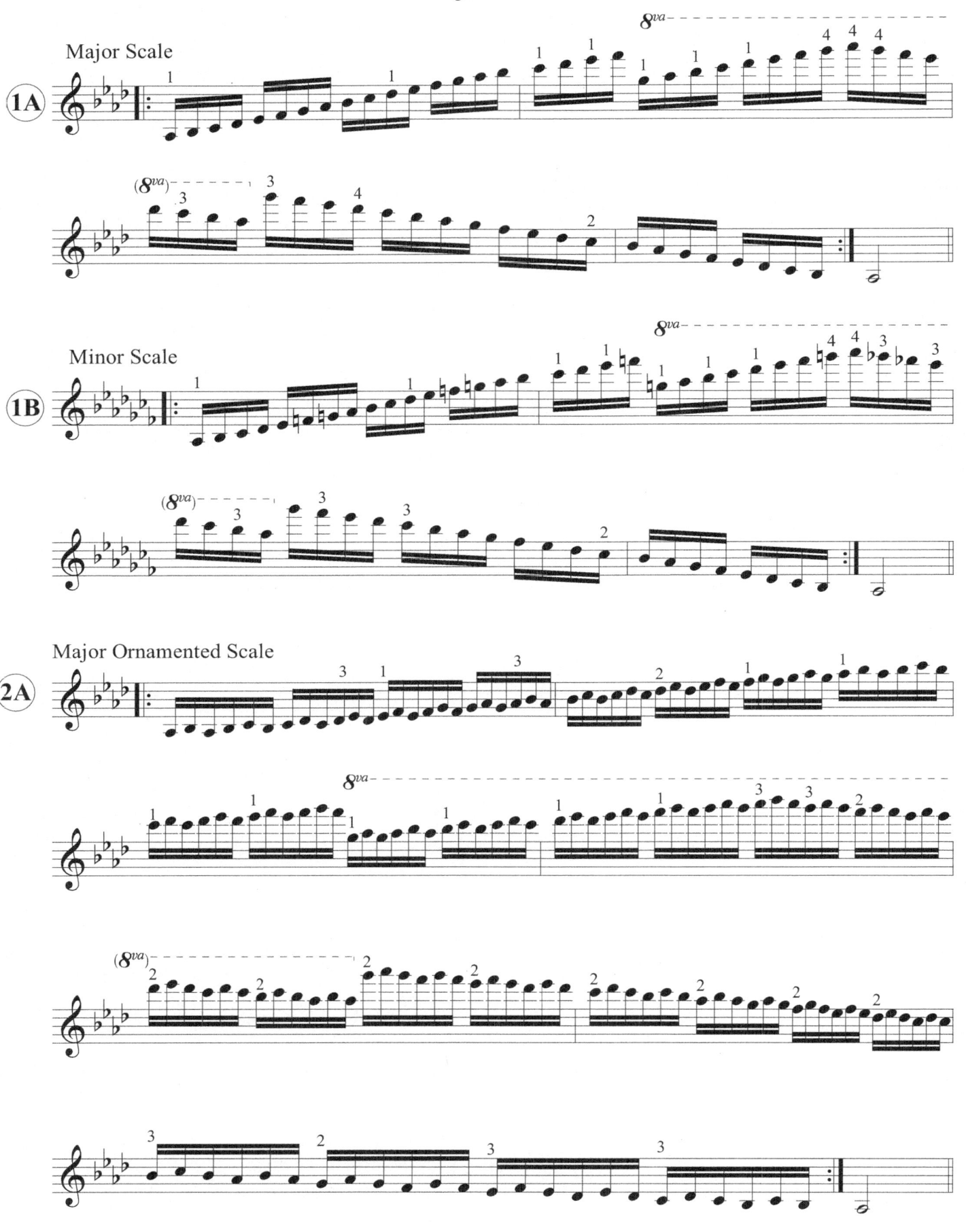

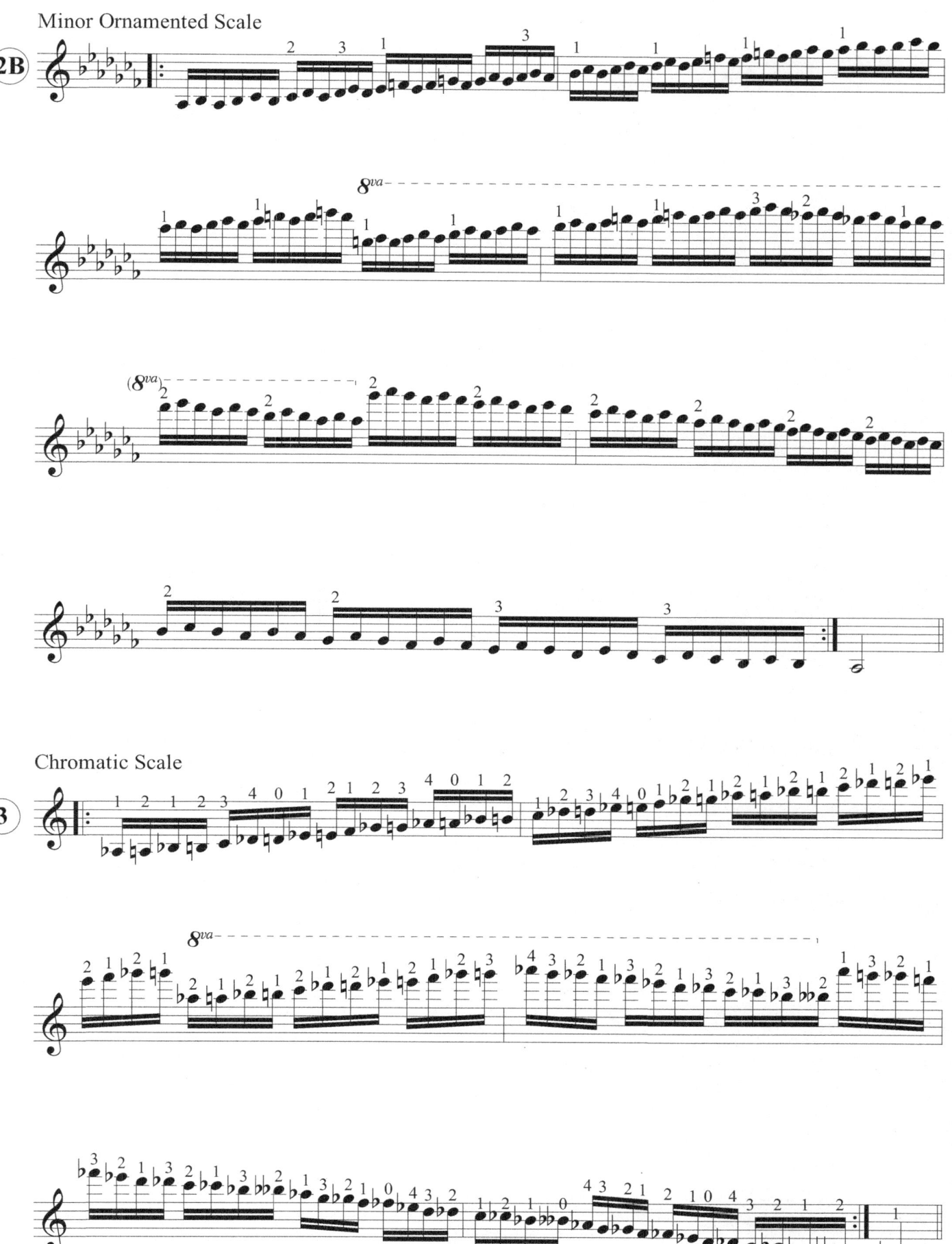

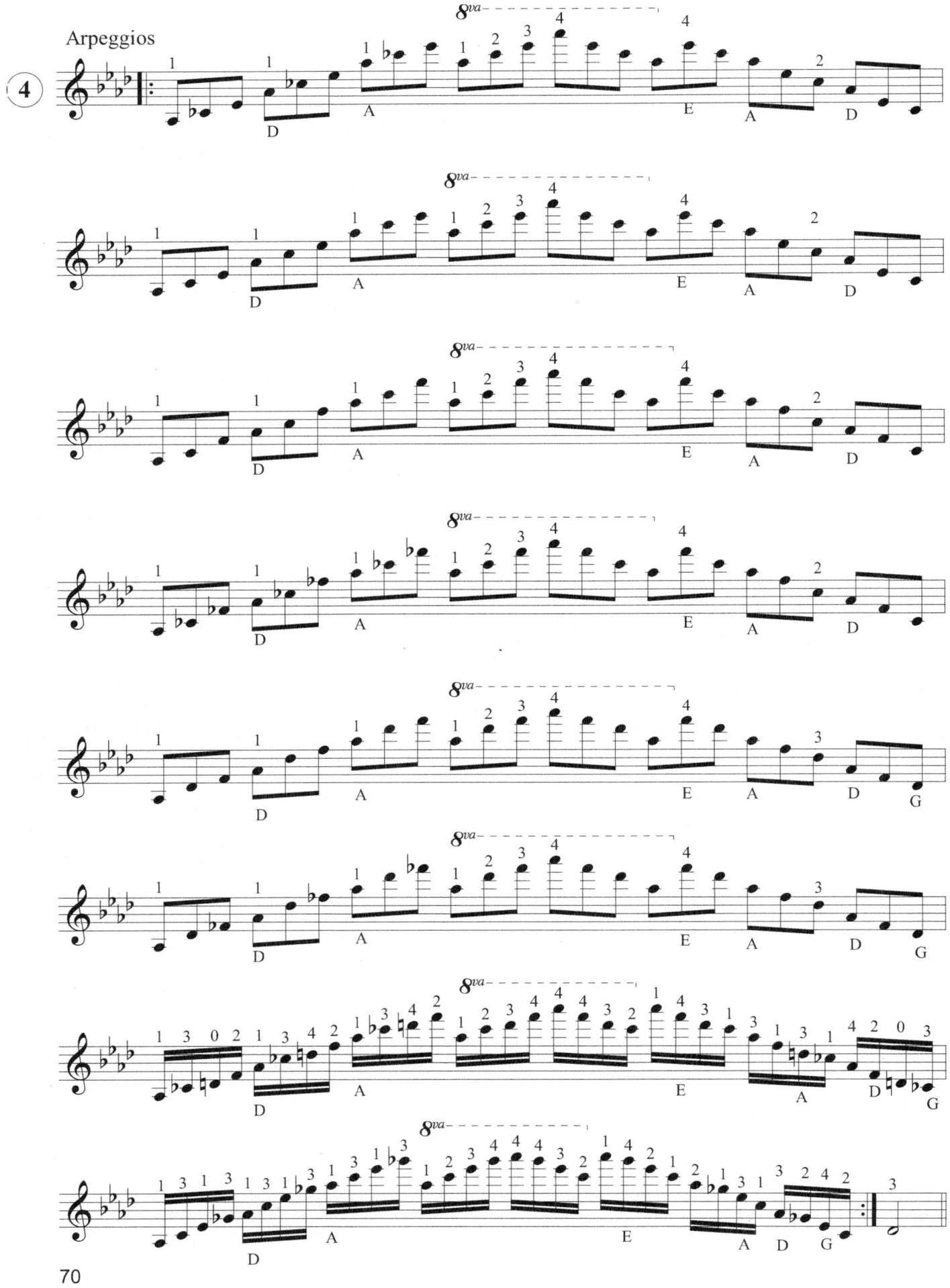

A Major / A Minor

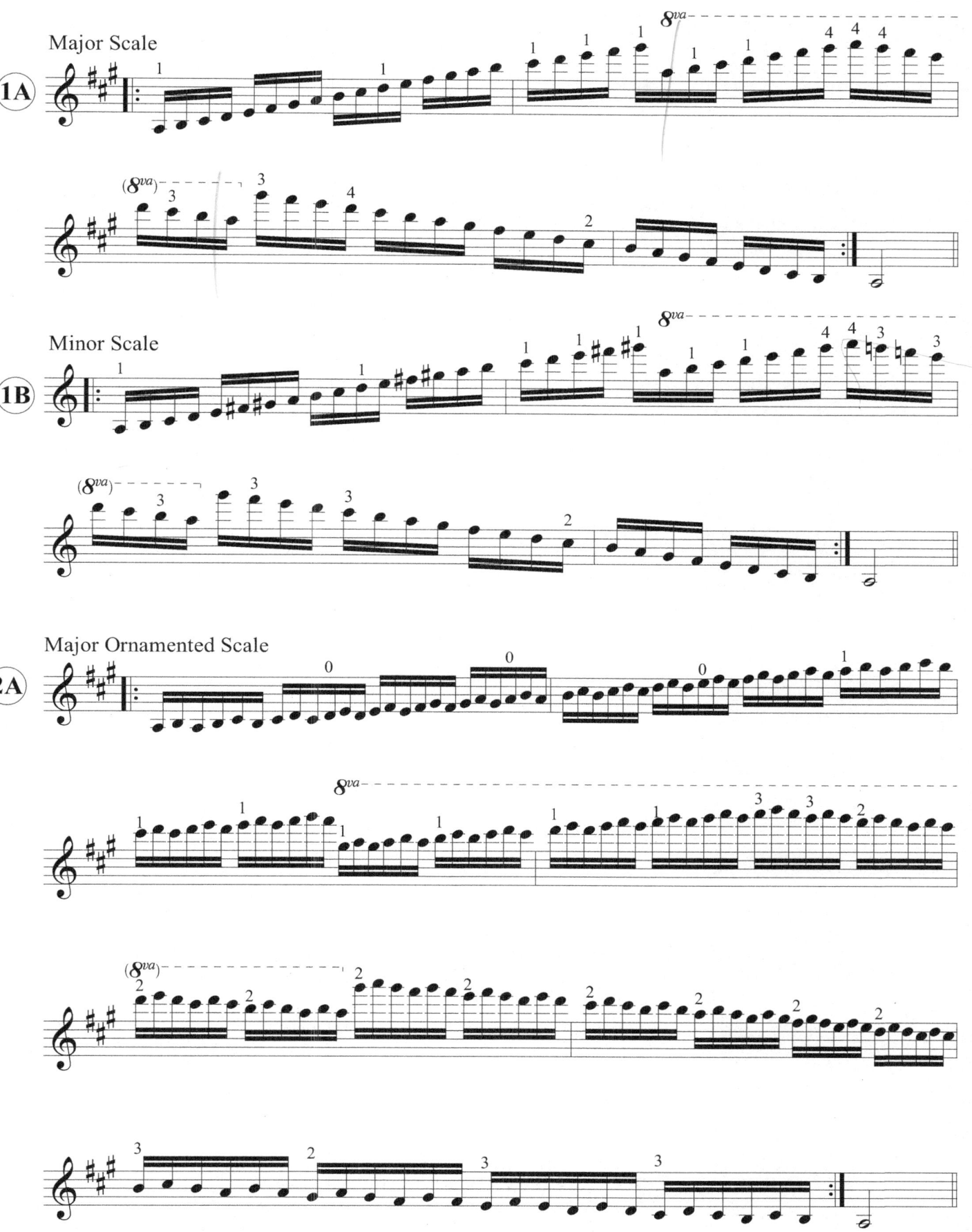

Arpeggios

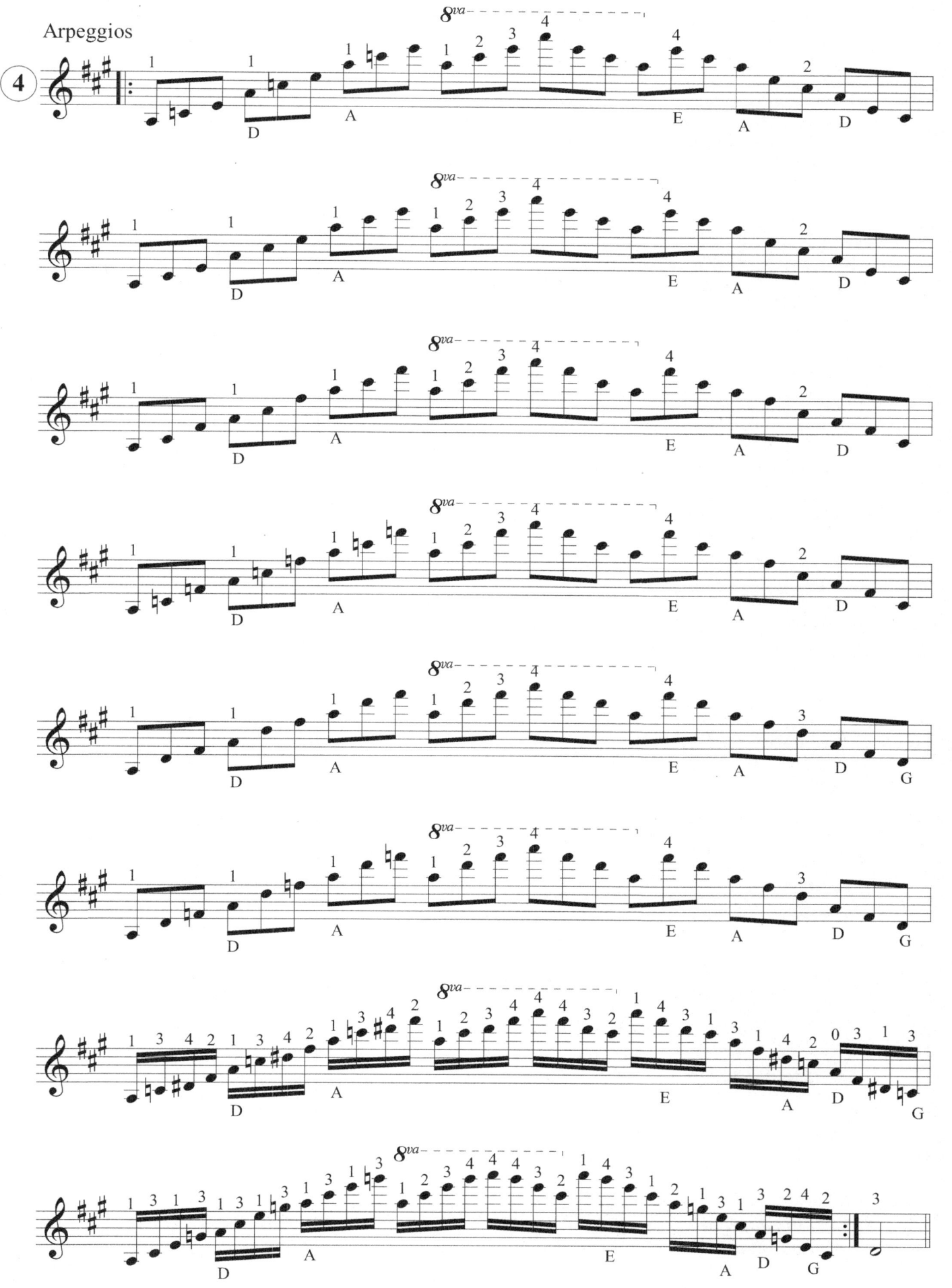

Bb Major / Bb Minor

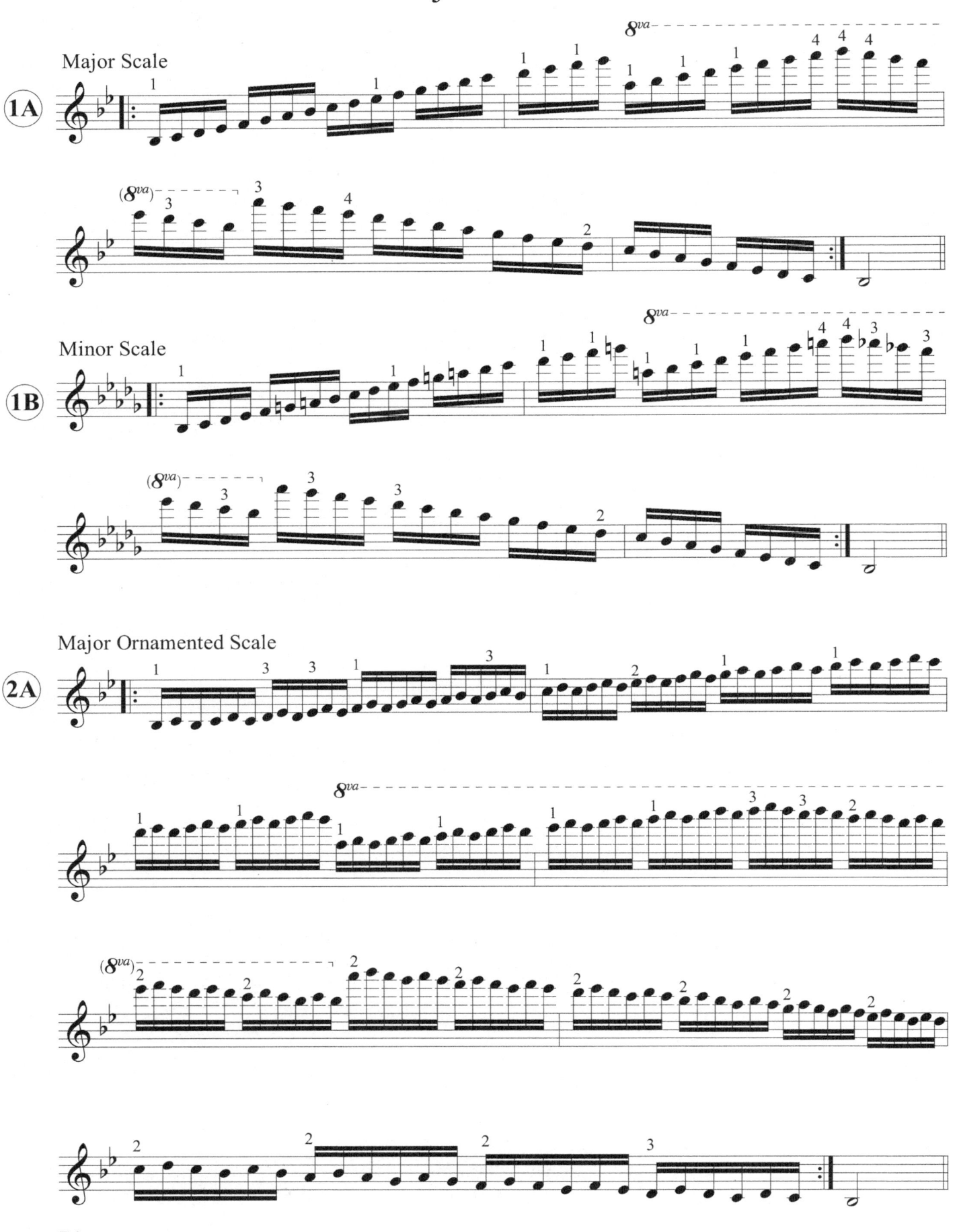

Minor Ornamented Scale

Chromatic Scale

B Major / B Minor

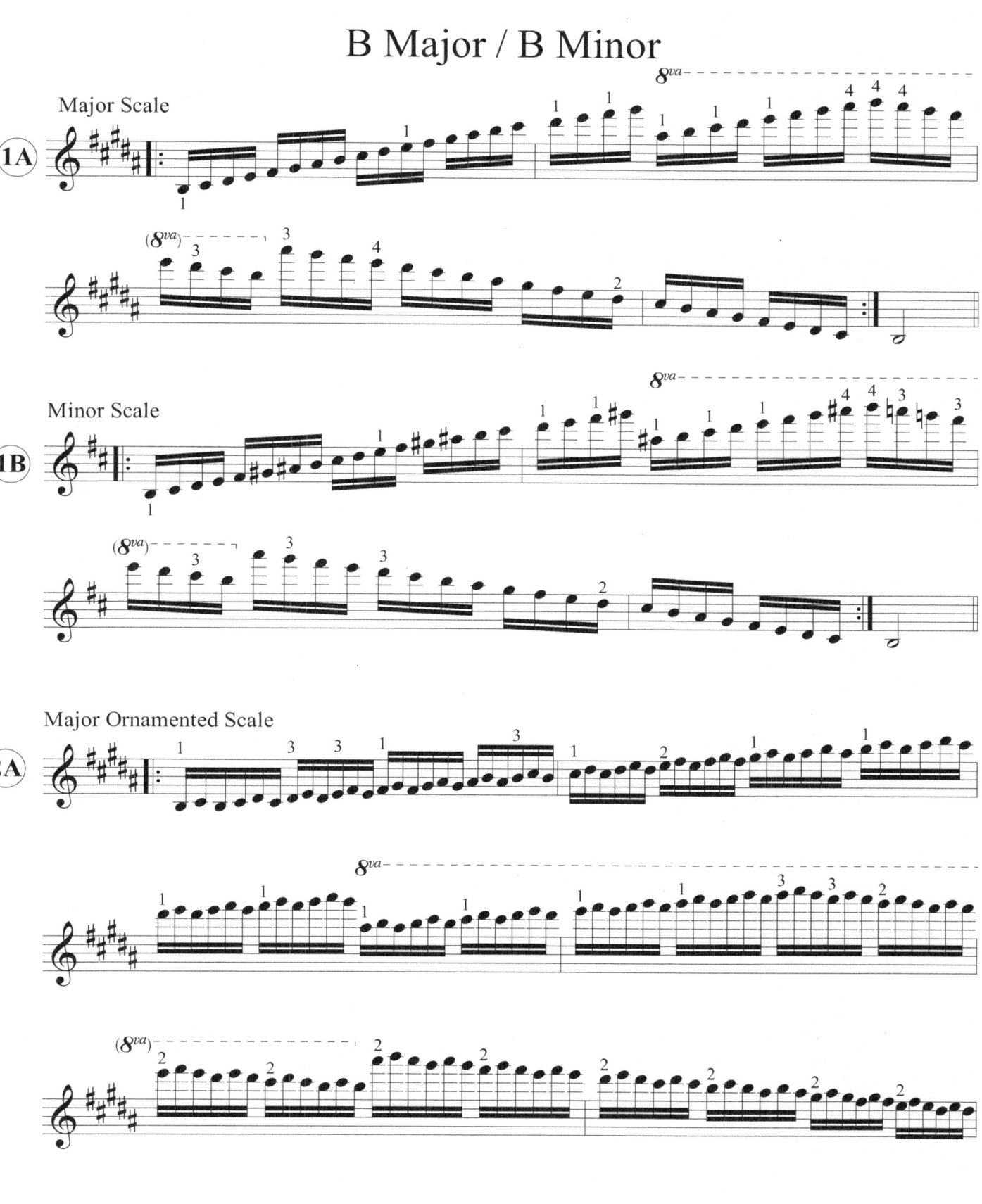

Minor Ornamented Scale

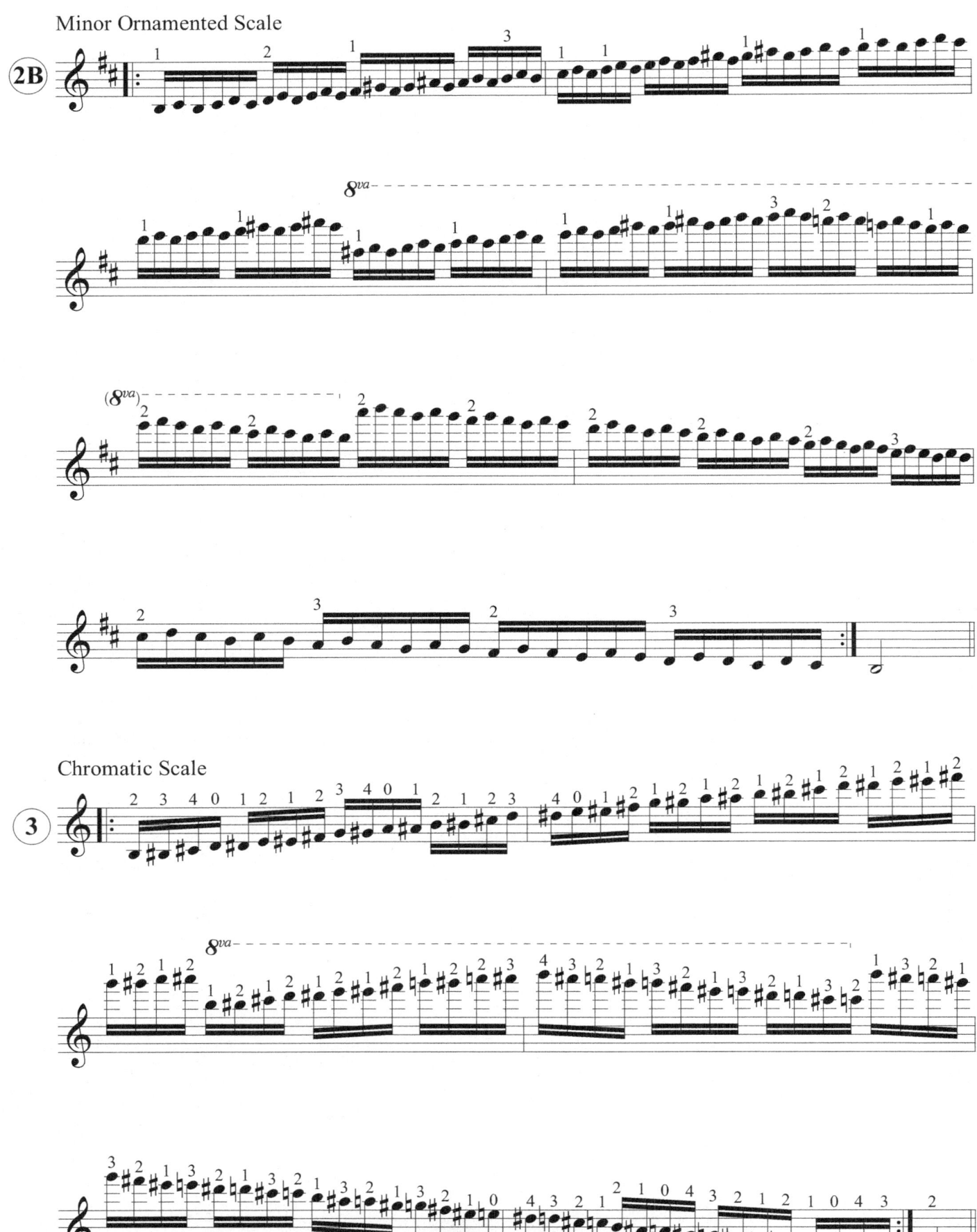

Chromatic Scale

Arpeggios

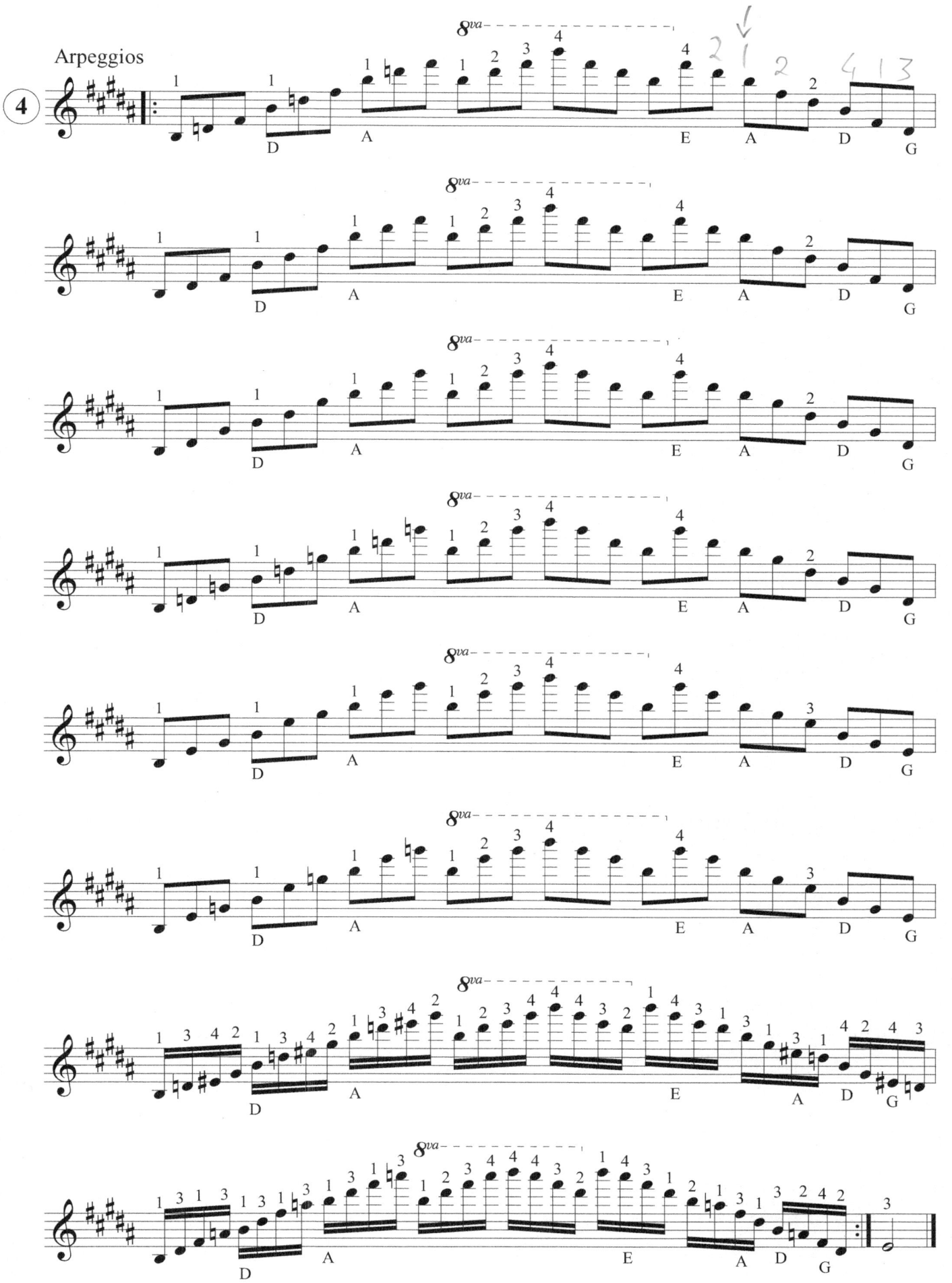

Printed in Great Britain
by Amazon